ALL NEW

Kitchen

IDEA BOOK

JOANNE KELLAR BOUKNIGHT

ALL NEW

Kitchen
IDEA BOOK

The Taunton Press

To Neil

Text © 2009 by Joanne Kellar Bouknight
Illustrations © 2009 by The Taunton Press, Inc.

The Taunton Press
Inspiration for hands-on living®

The Taunton Press, Inc.
63 South Main Street, PO Box 5506
Newtown, CT 06470-5506
e-mail: tp@taunton.com

Editor: Courtney Jordan
Copy editor: Valerie Cimino
Jacket/Cover design: Kimberly Adis
Interior design & layout: Kimberly Adis
Illustrator: Jean Tuttle

Library of Congress Cataloging-in-Publication Data
Bouknight, Joanne Kellar.
  All new kitchen idea book / Joanne Kellar Bouknight.
      p. cm.
  ISBN 978-1-60085-060-8
  1. Kitchens--Design and construction. I. Title.
  TX653.B67 2009
  643'.3--dc22
                            2008036275

Printed in the United States of America
10 9 8 7 6 5 4 3 2

The following manufacturers/names appearing in *All New Kitchen Idea Book* are trademarks: IKEA®

acknowlegments

THIS KITCHEN BOOK HAS BEEN COOKED UP BY MANY HANDS—hundreds of them, literally. There are interior designers and architects who designed these kitchens; craftspeople who built the products in them; builders, subcontractors, middlemen; homeowners and their kids; and photographers—the works.

My thanks to the designers, builders, and architects of the kitchens I worked with as we photographed their projects for this book, including Albano Appliance, Alward Construction, Deliberate Design + Architecture, Davids Killory Architects, Dirk Stennick Design, Kahlil Hamady of Hamady Architects, Dale and James Gould, Dail Dixon of Dixon Weinstein Architects, Vincent Petrarca of Tonic Design, Laura Kaehler, Joeb Moore, Deborah Emory, and Marie Louise from *Fine Cooking's* Cookstalk forum. I am grateful to the homeowners who opened their homes to us for photo shoots. Refer to the credits in the back for photographers and designers; please accept my apology for any omissions.

Special thanks to the photographers for our photo shoots—Ken Gutmaker, Hulya Kolabas, Randy O'Rourke, and James West—and to the photographers who took most of the remaining photos: David Duncan Livingston, Olson Photographic, Eric Roth, James R. Salomon, Brian Vandenbrink, Scot Zimmerman, and *Fine Homebuilding* magazine editors Brian Pontolilo, Charles Miller, and Charles Bickford.

The heart and soul behind this book is The Taunton Press, which for more than thirty years has been both inspiration and resource for information about designing and building kitchens. For years, whenever I've needed information about anything to do with houses (kitchens and cooking, especially), I head over to Taunton's website or my bookshelves of Taunton books and magazines, and I sit down for a close read or a quick look-see. The Taunton staff is high quality from head to toe, and my thanks to them for their wisdom, persistence, and deep-down generosity. In particular, many thanks go to my editor, the thorough, patient, and amazingly cheerful Courtney Jordan, and to senior editor Erica Sanders-Foege, who came to me with the project. In addition, my thanks to Alison Wilkes, Lucy Handley, Wendi Mijal, Valerie Cimino, Sandy Mahlstedt, Kimberly Adis, Jean Tuttle, and Peter Chapman (for old times' sake).

As with my other books and with every aspect of my life, from dawn to way past midnight, I thank my volunteering colleagues, my friends, and my family—both near and far—for being there in many ways, from granting forgiveness for forgotten birthdays to taking over tasks I normally do, and for telling kitchen stories.

My greatest thanks and love go to my husband, Neil, who works harder than anyone I know, but always has time to give me advice and support, and to our sons, Sebastian and Cornelius, who were little boys when I started my first kitchen book. They spent so much time in the kitchen then, washing dishes for hours . . . and hours.

contents

introduction

IT'S BEEN A PERFECT STORM OF DEADLINES in our house this year, what with me working on this book and our older son working on college applications. At one point during this intense time, it struck me that making a new kitchen is a lot like applying to college. There's all the research—reading, visiting, gathering opinions—then there's the winnowing down, the decision-making, and the waiting, and all of this occurs while you keep one thing in the back of your mind—the budget.

These days, finding the right college is all about fit, and what a good concept that is for kitchen design, too. If a high-school senior carries out his college search and selection with fit in mind—personal preferences, goals, and dreams tempered by reality—chances are good that come next fall he'll be in a college that suits him, rather than one that suits his best friend. It's the same with kitchens. Fit doesn't mean duplicating your neighbor's new kitchen. Nor does it mean copying the kitchen on the front cover of a glossy style magazine.

Why shoot for trendy or popular? Fit means the kitchen that's just right for you.

Finding a kitchen that fits is about mixing real life with the stuff of your dreams. It's a combination of existing conditions, aesthetic preferences, lifestyle, time, and budget, and it all starts with asking yourself some crucial questions: How do you want to use a new kitchen, how would you like it to look, and what are the elements that will go in it?

Consider the layout—in life size. Stage a virtual or actual walk-through of your cooking habits for all meals, from breakfast to holiday meals. You can chalk out a potential layout on a driveway, or use easy-to-remove gaffer's tape on the floor. Place real chairs around where you'd like to place a table or breakfast bar to see if you'll have the space you need to carry out typical kitchen tasks. This may seem silly at first, but you'll find that a life-size mockup is far easier to comprehend than a floor plan.

How involved will you be in the design and construction of your kitchen? Running

the show will take a strong constitution, patience, the ability to juggle several balls at once, and a knack for looking into the future. For many of us, designers and general contractors may be the best guides through this process—an experienced professional's years of experience can save hours of head-ache and a good deal of money. But that doesn't mean you won't benefit from staying engaged in the project and doing research. Your input will be crucial, so do your research.

As you consider the kitchen elements that are the right fit for you and your family, why not make saving energy and resources an important part of the picture? For green starters, site a kitchen addition to make the best use of sun, wind, foliage, and existing topography—e.g., work around rock rather than blast through it. Look into installing high-performance windows for solar gain and cross-ventilation. Ask about nontoxic paints, reclaimed wood, wood harvested from sustainable forests, and formaldehyde-free cabinetry. Another easy step in saving energy

is to shop for energy-efficient appliances and light fixtures. The most basic of all green tactics are building smaller and simpler.

After you determine what you are after, take your research on the road. Look in person at products. Find an appliance showroom that lets you test cooktops. Ask people, and read through online kitchen forums, but understand that for every person who raves about a certain countertop material, there is someone else who would love to take a sledgehammer to theirs. So trust your gut.

If you've made all the kitchen decisions based on how you live, what you love, and what you can afford, it is time to head into construction. If you did the legwork with your kitchen fantasies balanced with reality, I'll bet you designed the kitchen that is the best fit for you. And, as with the thousands of college freshman moving into their new dorms next fall, when you move into your new kitchen, you'll wonder how you ever lived without it.

style & layout

• • •

AS THE MOST POPULAR ROOM IN A HOUSE, THE KITCHEN NEEDS STYLE AND SUITABILITY. The style of a kitchen makes a lasting impression, and you want that impression to be one that pleases you. But how the space works when you are cooking and entertaining, not to mention as a living space, is a big part of a successful kitchen. Aesthetics and function should coexist in harmony. To achieve a blend of looks and function that suits your lifestyle and taste, take time to explore finishes, colors, and styles, and take a close look at the way you use the kitchen.

If time and money are short, quick style fixes can do the trick, but for a new kitchen or big renovation, do your research. Explore current design trends, if only to discover new products such as environmentally friendly paints and cabinets or the latest oven options. For a kitchen based on a specific historic style, look for cabinetmakers who work in that particular style, and find hardware, countertop materials, and lighting that complete the look.

As for layout, consider how the kitchen is used not only day-to-day, but all year long. What happens on a school morning or in the afternoon before a dinner party?

What sets a stylish, hardworking kitchen apart? Here, traditional cabinets painted a soft, buttery yellow provide a backdrop for the richly stained wood island. White marble countertops brighten the space, and the white gabled ceiling creates visual interest and allows the hood duct to look like a traditional chimney. Workspaces are situated in the tried-and-true triangle formation.

From the start of planning a new or renovated kitchen, think about how you'd like the kitchen layout to relate to the rest of the house and the outdoors. Those connections have a significant impact on how well the kitchen works and how comfortable it feels.

parts of the kitchen

●●● ALL THE ELEMENTS OF A KITCHEN CONTRIBUTE TO HOW IT LOOKS, so it's wise to make each design selection with the whole picture in mind. Cabinets are prime purveyors of a kitchen's style. If a traditional look is the goal, a purist may insist on face-frame cabinets with inset doors and drawers, but it's also possible to achieve a traditional look with flush overlay doors on frameless cases. Never underestimate the power of hardware to influence style, as offbeat pulls can liven up traditional cabinets and solid brass bin pulls can add gravitas to simple off-the-shelf cabinets.

Countertops set style in terms of material type, color, reflectivity, and edge profile. A huge, honed (matte) slab of marble set on a massive wood skirt and stout legs will add years—centuries—and a European aura to a farmhouse-style kitchen.

Appliances are essential to a kitchen's function, but they also play a role in establishing style. You can hide the refrigerator and dishwasher with panel covers that match the cabinetry and select a traditional range, such as a refurbished early 20th-century model or a cast-iron European range. Consider contrast, too. For example, a big stainless-steel range can add an industrial air that suits the modern aesthetic just as well as a traditional style. Sinks and faucets add style in a subtler way—unless you're aiming for a tall, restaurant-style faucet, which adds an overtly professional polish.

This contemporary kitchen is fitted with one-piece, flush overlay cabinet doors and black toekicks. The vibrant cabinet colors and orange-yellow walls add warmth and pizzazz.

This compact Manhattan kitchen has its only window facing a courtyard, so bright red cabinets and stainless-steel appliances help magnify the light and add spark to the small space.

With a traditional face-frame design and inset doors and drawers, these dark colonial-green cabinets are given a modern makeover with touches of stainless steel in the wall ovens and brushed nickel pulls.

This polished zinc serving bar maintains the kitchen's cool and soothing color palette of white, grays, and natural wood while introducing a new material that contrasts nicely with the matte wood and marble surfaces.

The dark tones of this kitchen's exotic sapele cabinets and brown painted walls stand out against the clean, white palette in the main living space of this modern house.

style overview

● ● ● IT'S FUN TO TAKE A LOOK AT THE LATEST KITCHEN TRENDS, but what really counts is what style feels right to you. Design a kitchen that makes you feel comfortable and reflects your personal taste. Do you like the serenity, substance, and warmth of the Craftsman style, or do you prefer the hard surfaces and gleam of a professional-style kitchen? Or do you crave a kitchen that Marie Antoinette would have loved (assuming she ever set foot in one)? It may seem easier to pick and choose a mix of styles for the various kitchen parts, but with every style you introduce, there is more to juggle conceptually. If your goal is to adhere to a certain style, it makes sense to understand what components—color, materials, surfaces, lighting—will help you achieve that particular look. Architectural books on the fashions of certain historical periods are a great source of inspiration, but you can also search for styles online as well. See the Resources on p. 214 for books and online sources about historical style.

From the stained
black concrete floor
to the high-velocity
hood, this kitchen
is unequivocally
modern. Regularly
spaced recessed
lights, a painted
brick wall, stylish bar
chairs, and lightly
grained marble
countertops add
subtle patterns and
textures.

FACING PAGE
Mixing traditional and
modern materials
gives this North
Carolina kitchen a
cozy, contemporary
look. Modern seating,
streamlined cabinets,
and glossy stainless
steel and polished
granite surfaces work
well with the traditional
wood flooring, island
cabinetry trim, and
comfy chairs in the
screened porch.

RIGHT Traditional
details give this kitchen
the look of a 19th-
century English manor.
Framed cabinets are
fit with inset doors
with butt hinges and
drawers with bin pulls.
Symmetry at and
around the range adds
to the formal look.
Ornate corner legs
give the semblance of
bottom trim, but offer
the convenience of
a toespace.

• traditional style

"Traditional" isn't a specific style like Arts and Crafts or French Provincial, but when that moniker is applied to a kitchen, it conjures up pendant lights, paneled doors, natural materials such as wood, tile, and stone, and articulated details, such as crown molding or beadboard. Comfort and warmth are key aspects of traditional kitchens. Specific styles hinge on the particulars, such as inset quartersawn oak doors on Shingle-style cabinets. A seriously traditional or country kitchen will have an unfitted look, with furniture-style legs and countertops of varying heights rather than banks of same-size cabinetry with modern toespaces. Traditional cabinets are wood, and finishes can range from paint and stain to a barely-there transparent rubbed wax. Dark wood floors are a favorite in today's traditionally styled kitchens.

FACING PAGE The strong contrast between dark blue cabinets and white woodwork gives this large kitchen a bright and airy appearance. Windows instead of wall cabinets let in natural light and reveal a lovely garden view.

BELOW Elegance and custom-crafted details define this large, traditional kitchen. Keys to achieving the look: complexly profiled trim, inset frame-and-panel doors and drawers with bin pulls and knobs, and columned feet.

The oversized brackets supporting the countertop and wall cabinets is an eye-catching detail in this traditional kitchen.

Modern appliances and light fixtures abound in this kitchen, but the traditional details—the elaborate cornice, divided-lite cabinetry doors, bin pulls, and ornately carved table legs—give a lasting impression.

• modern style

Modern with a capital M most often calls to mind unadorned detailing, smooth surfaces, recessed lighting, and full-flush doors in frameless cabinets, often with tall, Euro-style toespaces. Gleaming, man-made materials such as stainless steel, glass tile, linoleum, and composites may be the finishes of choice in a modern kitchen, but traditional materials and matte finishes can easily take on a modern cast if designed with clean, linear details. Play up a modern kitchen with a starkly sculptural faucet, a smooth cooktop, and a barely-there range hood.

ABOVE The clean lines of this modern kitchen are still welcoming. Shiny stainless-steel countertops pop against the dark cabinets, and the golden-hued wide-board wood floor adds warmth.

LEFT Face-frame cabinets are often traditional in style, but the narrow frames on these cabinets make for a modern look. Angular wire pulls, lever sink handles, and a textured, geometric backsplash tile add to the contemporary feel.

LEFT Black countertops and backsplash anchor this modern kitchen. There's no trim on the island, but wall cabinets have a tall toekick. The small bank of red cabinets and red chair cushions give the room a splash of color.

ABOVE Wood tones against shades of blue make a winning combination. A patchwork of large glass tiles in various blue and lilac hues is echoed on the backsplash in a slightly smaller scale.

• eclectic style

If your kitchen leans more toward an eclectic blend of styles rather than one overriding fashion, try to keep an overall sense of harmony and balance. For example, pair sleek stainless-steel appliances with beaded-panel cabinetry and ornate crown molding, or hang an elaborate chandelier over a starkly modern breakfast bar.

Color or texture can unify different style elements, such as white face-frame cabinets with a white sheet-glass backsplash. On the other hand, you may like to mix and match styles, colors, and textures for contrast.

ABOVE This mix-and-match kitchen combines traditional frame-and-panel doors with modern frameless cabinet cases. Mosaic glass tiles add spice to a neutral color palette of brown, tan, cream, and white.

LEFT Wood-paneled cabinets and a white marble countertop could suggest a traditional style, but stainless-steel hardware and stools, and the abundant use of turquoise, steer this kitchen in a decidedly eclectic direction.

ABOVE Modern cabinets—flat-panel flush overlay with wire pulls—combined with muted colors, open shelving, an exposed ceiling, and a wood floor give this eclectic kitchen a traditional flavor, too.

STYLE UPDATES

f budget and time constraints don't allow for substantive changes, small fixes are the ideal solution. Fit cabinets with new hardware or paint one wall of the room a different color—warm gray? Tuscan red?—or brighten a breakfast nook with bold wallpaper. Replace a flush-mounted fixture with a period

chandelier for instant glamour, or install surface-mounted puck lights under wall cabinets to brighten workspaces. A new backsplash of glass tile or stainless steel, or even a coat of bold paint, can give a kitchen an instant face-lift. Your kitchen will take on a whole new look with just a few effective changes.

What a difference paint makes to a kitchen! Three bright colors—lime, sunflower yellow, and lemon yellow—jazz up old cabinets and contrast nicely with the white backsplash and gray floor. A Roman blind echoes the color combinations.

a working layout

●●● WHILE YOU MAY BE ABLE TO TOLERATE A CABINET STYLE THAT DOESN'T REFLECT YOUR PERSONALITY, it's really tough to live with a kitchen that is difficult to cook in. If it is a hassle to make a cup of coffee in the morning and you can't face coming home and whipping up a meal, it may be a sign that your kitchen isn't functioning the way you need it to. As you reinvent your existing kitchen or dream up a custom kitchen design in a new house or addition, consider making space for more than one cook and possibly incorporating more than one set of appliances. Look for ways to add eating space and workspace in or near the kitchen, so that telecommuting for work, paying bills, and doing homework can happen side by side with meal prep. Think about the connection between cook and helpers or guests—does the cook want to prepare foods facing a wall, a window, or the rest of the kitchen? Take the opportunity to assess your family dynamic and do what works for you.

FACING PAGE LEFT
Kitchen task areas are tucked into their own alcoves in this elegant kitchen. The main prep countertop is directly opposite the range, so one person can easily go back and forth. The wide aisle allows two cooks to work comfortably opposite each other. The range alcove makes hood ventilation more efficient.

FACING PAGE RIGHT
This secondary workspace houses the kitchen's main oven, and a deep countertop provides room for small appliances and a bit of workspace. Corners of this hardworking space are trimmed with metal for durability and a clean, crisp look.

ABOVE The highly-functional layout of this kitchen offers two generous spaces for cooking with the sink equidistant from both stations. Wall ovens have ample countertop space beside them, and the range is flanked by two countertops. The fridge is close at hand but just a step out of the fray.

Even a large kitchen like this one can offer an efficient layout. The prep sink is opposite the cooktop, and the refrigerator and freezer are just a few steps away but easy to reach from the eating area. A portable cutting board makes it easy to transfer food to the cooktop.

RIGHT Most small kitchens make for tight working quarters for two cooks, but this compact kitchen is open-ended, making movement from either side easy and convenient.

• the kitchen triangle

Tie the major workspaces together with the kitchen triangle. The refrigerator, oven/cooktop or range, and sink comprise the major points of the triangle. The spaces between them—countertops or aisles—comprise the legs. Secondary appliances and prep areas such as a microwave, warming oven, baking station, and prep sink should fit as close to the triangle as needed. Two cooks? Two triangles. Ideally, the refrigerator is close to a landing space that can be used for groceries (going in) and dinner ingredients (coming out). The main sink should be close to the landing space and, hence, fairly close to the refrigerator. The cooktop requires space on each side and an adjacent prep area or possibly one across a narrow aisle on an island. The triangle makes the major tasks of food preparation, cooking, and cleanup an efficient process, so that you can get a meal on the table with ease and little fuss.

Two cooks can work easily in this open kitchen. There are several countertop workspaces to choose from, as well as wide-open circulation and immediate access to the eating area.

• beyond the triangle

Don't feel constrained by the concept of the kitchen triangle. Coloring outside the lines may be just what's required in your kitchen. Multiple cooks and appliances make layouts more complex. What's most important to consider is providing sufficient countertop space where it's needed—a cooktop needs not only landing space on each side but also enough space for prepping. An island is a good solution if there isn't room on each side of the cooktop. An additional sink allows you to wash and drain fruits and vegetables away from the main cooking action and also gives you a place to put dirty pots and pans so that they are out of the way. Two refrigerators (perhaps one is a drawer fridge) can cut down on foot traffic when cooking gets going.

FACING PAGE
Separating ovens from the island cooktop enlarges the cooking area but provides flexibility when there are two cooks in the kitchen. The raised island countertop keeps onlookers safe from food splatters but close enough to help with food preparation.

RIGHT Although there's a fair amount of room in this urban studio kitchen, the working triangle of refrigerator-range-sink is deliberately tight so that there is more room to eat and congregate.

Placing the microwave oven away from the cooking triangle allows easy access without blocking major cooking preparation. The expansive island countertop is shared by both cooks and non-cooks.

• space accommodations

A solo cook might well prefer a galley kitchen of two facing rows of cabinets with appliances and a 38-in. aisle with an island for eating, prepping, and watching. Two cooks will prefer wider aisles—42 in. to 48 in.—that allow appliances to open with ease. Doubling up on appliances might be the ticket for a kitchen with multiple cooks, with a major sink and

prep sink, two dishwashers, separate cooktop and oven, and even separate fridge and freezer, or supplemental refrigerator drawers near the eating area and out of the cook's path. Remember that even if a single cook is the everyday norm, little kids love to help and big kids may need to aid the chef, especially when big meals are in the making.

UNIVERSAL DESIGN

universal design refers to design for people of all ages and physical abilities. For wheelchair users, aisles in the kitchen should be at least 5 ft. wide, and there should be lower workspaces that do not have base cabinets. Additional guidelines include increasing the width of landing spaces beside refrigerators, cooktops, and ovens (a wall oven is a great solution). Make storage easy to access, select easy-to-use appliances and hardware, and keep ergonomics In mind. The added benefit of building with universal design in mind is that kitchens with a variety of countertop heights and storage options are in fashion. Be sure to check out the Resources section (p. 214) for more information and sources regarding universal design.

ABOVE This kitchen accommodates cooks and diners. Two identical sinks at the window allow for food prep and cleanup. The table in the center of the room pulls double duty as prep and dining space.

RIGHT A wide aisle like this one allows two cooks to work in the kitchen without getting tangled up. There is enough space to open drawers on both sides and still have room to walk in between.

integrate
the kitchen

●●● THANKS TO EFFECTIVE COOKTOP VENTILATION and a change in family dynamics, the kitchen has come out of the shadows and into top billing in today's homes, but it's still important to carefully consider its relationship to the rest of the house and to the outdoors. Linking the kitchen to living areas can be as simple as carving out a single opening to make a pass-through, or it can be the wholehearted commitment of wedding cooking and living spaces into a great room, where cooking, homework, and socializing are done together. Distinguish the kitchen by a change in materials on floors and walls, or by changing ceiling heights. Blend the kitchen—not an easy task, what with the equipment-heavy nature of the beast—into its surroundings by using compatible materials and colors. Hide appliances behind panels that match the cabinetry. Build in pocket doors that can enclose the kitchen during a gathering or after the cooking is done.

To enjoy dining alfresco, the easier it is to get outdoors, the better. This modern kitchen provides a direct route, and an abundance of windows allows cooks to enjoy the landscape all year long.

ABOVE Not entirely open to the house, but not entirely closed— that's an ideal layout for many kitchens. A bank of base cabinets makes a half wall topped by a wide countertop, but wall cabinets are left out to connect the space to adjacent rooms.

LEFT Renovating a century-old house provided the opportunity to open up this kitchen to the rest of the house by way of a framed opening in a bearing wall. Now the cook can have an eye on the cooktop and arriving guests.

An island is a dynamic addition to any kitchen, providing space for food preparation and plating a meal. Washing up at this island sink offers a view of the adjacent breakfast corner and workspace as well as the fish pond and woods beyond.

With high ceilings that open up to the second floor and access to dining and living spaces, this compact modern kitchen appears quite spacious. Parents making dinner and kids doing homework across the room can talk easily, and when it comes time for entertaining, the kitchen is an extension of the party.

In a tiny hillside house near San Francisco, the second-floor kitchen has the best views of the city, so it's a gathering space day and night. Keeping kitchen walls to a minimum makes the house seem bigger.

In this small Manhattan apartment, shoji-style doors neatly separate kitchen sights, sounds, and smells from the rest of the house without taking up precious space.

LEFT There's often a good reason to separate the kitchen from the dining area, and a pass-through can help bridge the spaces. This deep cutout provides a wide counter for dishes, great when it comes to serving and cleanup, and houses a microwave. On the dining side, built-in cupboards provide storage space.

ABOVE A variety of levels sets rooms apart without isolating them, as in this coastal house. The kitchen is just a few steps up from the family room. A half wall, slightly higher than the countertops, shields kitchen functions from those lounging below.

In a California kitchen, there's no question that the sunny outdoors should be just a step away. The sliding-glass door in this kitchen opens to a deck that's kept semi-private with a louvered screen and an overhead trellis.

outdoor view

●●● A GREAT VIEW MAKES A KITCHEN OPEN AND INVITING, whether it is a scene of the backyard or distant mountains, a lake, or the sea. Can the chief cook see that view when preparing a meal? Consider where to locate a warm-weather outdoor eating space so that it's a convenient few steps from the kitchen. A screened porch will be in constant use if it's adjacent to the kitchen, but will be simply a sitting room if not.

RIGHT An oversized window connects the kitchen to a screened porch, making conversation and transfer of food and dirty dishes an easy process. Having a sink at hand even allows porch-sitters to refill a glass of water.

BELOW A screened porch extends the kitchen and dining room three seasons of the year, especially if it's easy to serve food on it. An operable window adjacent to a cooking space or workspace makes it happen.

Plenty of sunshine and a great view trump the need for more storage space, so consider going without a bank of wall cabinets and adding a corner window instead, as in this country-style kitchen.

Why even have walls?
This house in the
Pacific Northwest
has panel doors that
slide out of sight to
open up the kitchen
to an amply covered
outdoor seating area.

GREEN
CONSIDERATIONS

t hinking green in the kitchen helps save money, energy, and health. Consider cabinet, countertop, and flooring materials that demand less energy to manufacture and don't need to be installed and maintained with harsh chemicals. Salvaged materials are great for kitchens too. Keep in mind that the kitchen uses energy at a faster clip than any other room in the house because of appliances, so look into purchasing new models—and smaller ones, if possible—to save on energy consumption. Make recycling part of everyday life by including space for collecting and sorting empty food containers. Rely on natural light—and fresh air—as much as possible by incorporating lots of operable windows, and use energy-efficient light fixtures where artificial light is necessary.

ABOVE This kitchen space brings the outdoors into a house in the city. Its floor-to-ceiling windows allow for abundant light and a view into a walled garden, a private place to have a quiet meal and grow herbs and vegetables.

RIGHT The biggest way to save energy is by thinking small, as in this cozy house built for two. Prep, cooking, and cleaning are all handled in the galley kitchen, and a drop-leaf table adds another surface space for dining or prepping when needed.

the kitchen island

● ● ●

A KITCHEN WITHOUT AN ISLAND IS A RARE BEAST THESE DAYS, even if it's a small island that could be swallowed up by the tide. An island is a kitchen's multitasker, often doing double, if not triple, duty for busy cooks. The contemporary island owes its status in kitchens to its great-grandmother, the colonial keeping room, where the household would gather around the broad kitchen table to cook, eat, talk, and tend to schoolwork and handiwork. In the same way, a farmhouse kitchen's broad kitchen table is where numerous tasks take place throughout the day.

Nowadays in urban and suburban kitchens, the island performs a similar function on a smaller scale. If intermediate countertop space for more cooks and improved efficiency is needed, an island fits the bill. A sink in the island allows for washup, stowing dirty dishes, and rinsing food. An island can also bridge the gap between refrigerator and cooktop, acting as prep space. Once dinner is underway, prep space can be transformed into a casual dining area.

An island can be so much more than a set of cabinets topped with a counter. Adding appliances and fixtures like a dishwasher, microwave, wine rack, stowaway garbage can, or freezer can make an island a dynamic space in your kitchen. Take the time to really think through what its dimensions should be, where to position it, how to configure and finish all its sides, how to light it, and what its height should be.

A kitchen island can handle a multitude of tasks if it's designed for versatility. The quartersawn oak base of this island is narrow to accommodate seating yet wide enough for storage. The countertop materials and heights vary, with a marble surface for pastry-making and dining that sits slightly lower than the island's bamboo butcher block.

island
dimensions

● ● ● WHILE THERE'S NO SET ISLAND SIZE, efficiency and comfort guide island height and placement. Where there's traffic, keep aisles between an island and base cabinets at least 4 ft. wide. Where there is one cook, the aisle can shrink to 40 in. wide or even less, while two cooks work best with a little more room, so a 42-in. to 60-in. aisle between the island and base cabinets is best. Allow at least 60 in. between an island and an adjacent dining table.

A narrow island functions best at one countertop level. A wide island can do the same or accommodate differing countertop heights for various functions—low for pastry-making and high for bar seating (see p. 66 for suggested countertop heights). An island with a healthy girth will force cooks to do more walking, so it may make sense to fill an especially large central space with two separate islands.

ABOVE A built-in island has to have electrical outlets, but figuring out where to put them can be tricky. This two-layer island with sapele cabinets and a granite countertop has a raised stainless-steel shelf that offers an out-of-the-way recess for receptacles.

RIGHT Before dinner, the island in this kitchen is the main food-prep space. When it is time to eat, the overhang on each side of the piece allows two to four people to dine comfortably.

Large and solid, this island is mindful of the details. Its recessed toespaces with corner legs give the substantial piece a bit of delicacy. There's seating space on the opposite side of the prep sink. Pendant lights provide task lighting for the entire workspace.

This long island has room for just about everything—seating at the ends, a substantial wine storage cabinet, and lots of prep space. Cutting boards are within easy reach so that no amount of slicing or dicing will damage the soft, face-grain countertop.

built-in island details

● ● ● BUILT-IN ISLANDS BRING SO MUCH ADDED BENEFIT TO KITCHENS, so make sure to consider all the little details during design. Built-in islands require electrical receptacles at code-required locations; don't let the placement and materials of these be a design afterthought. Instead, center them on architectural features and specify covers that harmonize with the kitchen design. Also be aware that any appliances or sinks located in islands need accompanying plumbing, wiring, or ductwork. The central position of an island can provide flexibility to an HVAC design, as it may accommodate more possibilities for return-air or supply ducting.

In terms of lighting, carefully consider the positioning and effectiveness of pendants, track lights, or recessed cans. Because an island is almost always used for food preparation or cooking, consider comfort when determining countertop overhangs and base design. If countertop overhangs are shallow, allow for toespace; if you like a chunky baseboard, allow the countertop to extend a bit more.

To accommodate utilities for a gas-fired cooktop, the center of this birch-veneered island rests on a recessed base faced in stainless steel. To lighten the apparent bulk of the island, and add a touch of whimsy, the ends are supported by legs.

ABOVE There's dining space directly across from this island, but the cook prefers to sit at the stainless-steel countertop, where there's room to prep vegetables or read a cookbook.

FACING PAGE Islands provide transition between cooking and living spaces, often with an informal dining area. These cushy bar-height chairs make the cantilevered island countertop an elegant and welcoming place to enjoy a meal.

Comfortable bar stools and a deep overhang create a much-used informal dining space out of this island, and the countertop is expansive enough to set an entire meal or act as serving space for a large dinner party.

• floating islands

Space, style, or budget may suggest that a movable island is the best choice for a kitchen. An antique kitchen worktable can be a flexible, stylish centerpiece for a traditional kitchen, and it offers a bit of open storage as well. A simple kitchen table set on high legs can also stand in as an island and be a place for food preparation, dining, and homework. Movable island furniture is also a good choice if it's not feasible to install the receptacles that a built-in island requires by code. Of course, such an island won't make a safe home for a mixer or food processor.

FACING PAGE Just because it's not a built-in doesn't mean an island is insubstantial. This massive island with a profiled white marble top is styled to look like a piece of antique furniture. The fanciful modern pendants overhead suggest this island is going to stay put.

BELOW A moveable island leaves a lighter footprint than a fixed island. It's easy to move when the occasion arises, and there's no need for it to have electrical outlets. There's plenty of storage space, and shelves are open and airy.

all about...
COOKING SAFELY ON AN ISLAND

@ cook who loves to be at the center of the action, working with friends and family around, will love the spotlight that a cooktop on an island brings. Just be aware of the need for a few commonsense safety precautions. Allow for an expanse of heatproof landing space on all three sides of the cooktop—at least 15 in. on the flanking sides, as well as a broad expanse or raised surface on the far side. A vertical barrier provides protection from spatters and steam and is also a perfect spot to plate a meal. The most efficient cooktop exhaust system is one with a range hood, which draws heat and grease upward and away. An integrated downdraft exhaust system is sufficient for cooking that is not typically a four-burner affair. A range hood with a gleaming surface or unusual shape can be a great design feature, and it also provides the lighting a cook needs over the range.

This multidimensional island has a lot going on. Range and hood with flanking countertops and base cabinets provide function and style, while columns and storage-filled column bases turn the whole piece into a room divider. The raised countertop in the center acts as a plating area and informal dining space.

multifunction islands

●●● AN ISLAND WEARS MANY HATS. Its several sides give cooks more than one place to prep, and it positions the meal-makers so that they can face each other, talk with onlookers, or look up for a view into another room or the outdoors. Prep space should be approximately 3 ft. to 6 ft. wide and 18 in. to 24 in. deep, but gauge your own work habits to set your own standards. Choose countertop materials to suit the island's tasks. If it will be used predominately as prep space, a solid surface is a serviceable choice. If aesthetics are a concern, a face-frame wood surface is a decorative alternative that gives an island's serving and eating space high style.

Plan a multilevel island if you'd like to separate tasks from one another, or if the cooks come in a wide range of heights. In fact, if small children will be working in the kitchen—whether as sous chefs, doing homework, or playing—it is a good idea to add a lower countertop for them that can then double as a bread- or pastry-making surface for adults.

TOP The island in this country house serves as prep and serving space, and accommodates standing diners. Storage space—shelves and doors on one side and drawers on the other—is hidden behind white cabinetry doors.

RIGHT The island is the centerpiece in this kitchen with a corner sink for convenient food prep.

The cabinets in this kitchen have classic, simple lines. But the island, with its generously curved countertop, ornate brackets, and rich gray color, provides a more elaborate design profile.

Island cooktops and sinks allow the cooking action in the kitchen to spread out, but also require careful attention to utilities. Power, fuel, and plumbing have to be routed through the floor structure, and a large hood is a must for adequate ventilation.

ISLAND APPLIANCES AND SINKS

the island can be the central spot for most of the appliances in the kitchen, whether set up on the working side of the island or the non-cook side. If the cooktop and wall ovens are positioned on a wall, think about having a microwave oven or warming oven in the island so that it's closer to the dining action, although this won't be a good choice if small children spend time in the kitchen. A below-counter refrigerator and freezer are perfect candidates for island duty

so that hungry family members can retrieve cold beverages or snacks without interfering with cooking tasks. A sink can make an island workspace much handier if there's sufficient space and available plumbing. Because an island is usually the focus of a kitchen, think twice about locating a big washup sink in the island unless there's a higher countertop to shield dirty dishes. An expansive island with nothing on the surface but open space will be a baker's delight.

FACING PAGE
Three thick slabs of marble wrap around a cabinet to make this kitchen island, which has a deep sink in the center, opposite the range for convenience. The cabinet back is painted black on the bar side. A luminous custom-made light fixture provides diffuse yet bright light for work or dining.

island storage

●●● THE ALL-SIDES-AVAILABLE FEATURE of an island allows for storage in several places and for different needs. Consider a combination of closed and open storage, fixed and pullout shelves, and drawers of all sizes. Turn non-storage sides into shelves or finish them with decorative panels, tile, or beadboard. Dedicate non-storage sides to dining space. Set aside certain storage areas on the prep side of the island for cooking gear. Dishes, placemats, and silverware should be kept on the dining side. This will keep everything you need at hand and everything you don't need out of your way. While a curved island can make for smoother traffic patterns, keep in mind that curved cabinetry is expensive and may reduce available storage space. The solution is easy: Curve the countertop, not the cabinets. The resulting countertop overhang can be a handy sitting spot if it's deep enough.

A narrow island makes a good design sense, as shallow shelves offer easy access to dishes and keep drawers at a comfortable depth. Topping it off, the countertop makes a perfect coffee bar.

Two slender bookcases not only offer cookbook space, but also give this island a substantial look and make the seating area cozier.

Plenty of drawers make for a highly functional island. A short overhang provides bar seating and the gray strip below the countertop is home to easy-reach outlets for small appliances.

dining &
work spaces

• • •

A HEART-OF-THE-HOUSE KITCHEN IS NOT ONLY HOSPITABLE TO THE
COOK OR COOKS, BUT IT ALSO GIVES GUESTS AND OBSERVERS A
PLACE TO SIT, EAT, AND SOCIALIZE. Dedicated space for eating in or near the
kitchen makes every meal a cozy affair with easy cleanup afterward. Adjacent dining
space is great for incorporating the kitchen into a dinner party and also makes sense
for people on the go who may need to eat and run.

Cooking style, family size, and how the kitchen connects to the rest of the house
determine how and where dining should be incorporated into the kitchen. In-kitchen
dining can be as casual as pulling up a few stools to a 36-in.-high countertop
overhang or as extensive as renovating a section of the room to accommodate a
breakfast nook or substantial dining table.

Besides eating, think about the other non-cooking tasks done in the kitchen.
Space for kids to do supervised homework is an added bonus of an eat-in nook.
You may be in that category of cooks who bake or tend long-simmering braises
while working at a computer or paying household bills. Keep in mind that these
workspaces should be sheltered from high-heat and
messy food preparation, but should allow for quick
access to what's cooking.

**It's convenient if not an outright
necessity to have dining space
in the kitchen, especially in
a Manhattan apartment like
this one. The versatile pullout
table allows one or two to eat
anywhere, and the inset stone
top makes it an ideal pastry-
making station. When dinner
is done, the table becomes a
workspace for paying bills or
doing homework.**

dining spaces

TABLE FOR EVERYDAY MEALS, so in-kitchen dining is the perfect solution. Make this space work for you by thinking about its size, location, and flexibility. Should dining accommodate just the kids or the whole family? Would you prefer dining away from food preparation or right in the thick of things? If the latter appeals, add an at-hand undercabinet refrigerator so diners can help themselves to drinks, or position the refrigerator and freezer in the area between cooking and seating.

How flexible do you want this space to be? Built-in counters and seats are great for staking a permanent claim, but movable furniture makes it easier when it comes time to make room for a bigger crowd or for accommodating the many cooks it takes to pull off a seasonal feast.

This black and white New England kitchen is as elegant and tasteful as its adjoining dining room, so there's no need to close it off.

LEFT The kitchen addition of this colonial country house maintains the original low ceiling. To create a sense of spaciousness, a high bank of cabinets was installed. It acts as a transition space between kitchen and dining area, and the raised portion keeps any dirty dishes in the sink out of view.

BELOW Two adjacent seating areas offer distinctly different dining options. The dining table with a wall-to-wall view of the city is the more formal of the two spaces. The bar stools at the island offer casual, chat-with-the-cook seating.

This rounded countertop is raised just an inch to distinguish it from the workaday surface around the sink. Chairs are moved aside when space is needed for dinner preparation or serving the meal.

An area with walls and individual windows—as opposed to the floor-to-ceiling windows flanking the space—creates a cozy niche for eating, especially a late supper or midnight snack.

With a cooktop and hood located at the end of this kitchen island, the cook has as lovely a view as the diners in this coastal kitchen, and serving dinner is a matter of a few quick steps.

• room for table and chairs

You may never miss having a formal dining room if there's room in the kitchen for a standard dining table and enough chairs for family and guests. In a kitchen with a great view, position the table and chairs close to the windows rather than crowding that space with cabinetry.

A dining alcove can be finished in softer, less durable materials than the rest of the kitchen—just like a formal dining room. In fact, for instant sophistication, consider adding sliding doors or shutters that can be closed or tucked away to unite cooking and dining.

Creating a cozy dining space just two steps up from a compact kitchen provides a bit of separation and a great view of the outdoors, as well as quick access to the kitchen area below and the herbs in the cook's garden.

A kitchen isn't often on the second floor, but that's where the best view is in this Bay Area hillside house. Dining a step down from the kitchen proper creates a subtle distinction between two spaces.

built-in dining nooks

●●● A BUILT-IN DINING NOOK ISN'T JUST FOR BREAKFAST ANYMORE. Such a space can easily become the most sought-after spot in the house. Benches make it easy to squeeze in that extra person. So you don't get too crowded, go with a 42-in.- to 48-in.-wide bench for two adults or three kids, with the top of the seat 18 in. off the floor. Make space allowances for cushions, keeping in mind that certain materials compress more than others. Allow 18 in. to 20 in. between the seat-back cushion and the edge of the table. This allows diners to slide into their seats easily, but keeps the table comfortably close for eating. A 30-in.-high table is standard, but you may want to raise or lower that standard slightly based on your own situation. To make it comfortable for people to slip in and out of a corner bench, consider rounding the corners of the table. Make use of the furniture in the nook for storage. Seldom-used items can be stored in benches. The enclosing walls become an instant art gallery with the addition of a few corkboards. Installing a few shallow shelves gives space for decorative kitchen items or cookbooks.

ABOVE A small kitchen often depends on a breakfast bar to accommodate informal dining, but here a breakfast nook built into the back of the sink cabinet provides enough room for the whole family with the help of a few chairs.

RIGHT It's hard to imagine ever wanting to get up from the plump and comfy seats of this built-in dining nook, but when it's time to clear the table, there are storage drawers and flip-top bins under the cushions to stow games, puzzles, or newspapers.

FACING PAGE Gustav Stickley would approve of this built-in dining alcove with room for eight or more. Drawers are tucked under the seats, and wide ledges offer not only display and storage space, but also a comfortable buffer between diners and windows.

While this dining space is built into the walls, it is fit with freestanding pieces. Two off-the-shelf benches provide seating and the table is a living room corner table that's been retrofit with a large top that provides a deep overhang.

ABOVE At the moment, the small table in this kitchen provides enough room for a few people to gather for a quick bite, but the banquette is spacious enough to accommodate a larger table if necessary.

FACING PAGE A dining niche is the perfect spot for built-in bookcases, and the built-in bench in this kitchen offers space for dining, chatting, or reading. It can stand—or sit—alone if the table is moved.

BUILT-INS WITH MOVABLE PARTS

Sometimes a combination of built-in and movable furniture makes the perfect dining space in a kitchen. A built-in bench against the wall can seat one to three people with permanent storage space always available. When there's a crowd, a few more people can just pull chairs up to the table. A pedestal table allows easy access to a dining nook and if it is freestanding, the table can be removed to accommodate larger groups. As a bonus, movable furniture makes it easier to clean up.

breakfast bars

● ● ● BREAKFAST BARS ARE IDEAL FOR INFORMAL DINING AT ANY TIME OF DAY. Side-by-side seating is great for breakfast diners who are sharing the newspaper or working on a crossword puzzle together. Lunch and dinner diners can sit at the breakfast bar and not only talk to the cook, but see what's cooking as well. Bar heights should range from 36 in. to 48 in. You will want to make sure that the bar stools or chairs fit the height of the bar (see drawing on p. 66 for suggested combinations of countertop and seat heights). Stools are great for sliding under the countertop when not in use, while chairs add back support for long stints of sitting.

ABOVE All talk and all action are the hallmarks of this kitchen built to look like a high-style diner. The raised countertop keeps sink-based activity out of view and makes the perfect place to spread a buffet when entertaining.

FACING PAGE Here's a breakfast bar with views of the landscape outside and the handsome range niche right on the other side of the raised countertop. The wood countertop is meant for dining and serving, as there's plenty of prep space elsewhere.

Tall bar chairs are most comfortable when feet aren't left swinging. The low foot perches on these models make it easy to get in and out of the seat.

RIGHT A comfy bar stool provides ample leg room but keeps diners close to the counter. These stools have short backs that provide support while sitting and are low enough to push under the counter when not in use.

BELOW A breakfast bar allows diners and cooks to chat with ease, but also puts stacks of need-to-clean dishes out of view. This countertop is wide enough for table settings and is conveniently close to the sink for when the meal is done.

This simple breakfast bar and table combo is artfully detailed with a curved support screen and light fixture on the ceiling. Stools fit completely under the table to make room for food preparation.

COMFORTABLE DINING DIMENSIONS

Suggested depths are shown for sitting at various height countertops and for universal access seating, particularly wheelchairs. As a rule of thumb, the higher the countertop, the shallower the knee space required for diners.

COMFORTABLE DINING DIMENSIONS	COUNTER HEIGHT	KNEE SPACE DEPTH	WIDTH	SEAT HEIGHT
Table dining	28 in. to 30 in.	18 in.	24 in. per chair/stool	18 in. to 19 in.
Standard countertop height	36 in.	15 in.	24 in. per chair/stool	24 in. to 26 in.
Bar height	42 in.	12 in.	24 in. per chair/stool	30 in.
Universal design access for wheelchair	36 in.	15 in.	24 in.	NA

This breakfast bar gives diners the best seats in the kitchen. The arched portal frames the cooktop and provides the perfect place to watch the cook prepare a meal or plate a dish.

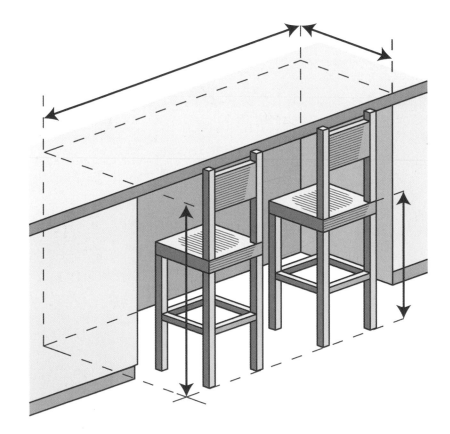

Behind this custom-made cypress breakfast bar, the cooktop and a sink are hidden. Stools pushed under the cantilevered bar top allow party guests to perch, stand, or lean.

ABOVE This breakfast bar with a edge-grain wood countertop makes an elegant place to dine or to chat while a meal is prepared. Fridge and storage are tucked into a butler's pantry at left.

LEFT When it's time to cook, the downdraft vent in this kitchen pops up to vent the cooktop and protect onlookers from splatters. During meals at the bar, the vent tucks away for streamlined dining, as shown.

all about...
SPACE TO HANG OUT

ometimes there's no need for a table to take up space when all you need is a place to sit. A comfy chair, couch, or built-in bench is perfect for when you want to curl up and read, talk, do homework, or, in the case of a window seat, enjoy the view. A larger bench can even double as sleeping space when visitors stay the night, and it's the best spot for snacking during a midnight refrigerator raid.

This charming and inviting window seat is home to friends or family, for meetings or conversation. There's plenty of room to pull up a table for an impromptu meal or when extra dining space is needed during the holidays.

ABOVE, TOP The kitchen is the heart of the house, so it makes sense to create comfy spaces where people can curl up and stay awhile. This cushioned built-in bench is perfect for working, relaxing, or taking a quick nap.

ABOVE, BOTTOM When kitchen, dining, and living space overlap, as in this small beach house, every piece of furniture performs double duty. The sofa is a place to sit and snack, and the kitchen table adds additional workspace for preparing a meal.

workspaces

● ● ● BECAUSE THE KITCHEN IS THE COMMAND CENTER for many households, a space set aside specifically for paying bills, keeping a calendar, doing homework, or even telecommuting can be essential. Look into how this space will make use of lighting and available support systems, and plan the location and layout accordingly. A useful workspace will probably require access to the Internet, phone lines, and electrical receptacles, so make sure cables and wires can be tucked away.

For a full-time workspace, meet the user's personal ergonomic requirements. A desktop computer system will require space above or below the desk for the computer itself. You can store the computer in a ventilated cabinet so that dust is kept to a minimum. And don't forget to dedicate space for the computer peripherals such as a printer, fax machine, scanner, or an all-in-one device, which would be perfect for space-saving in a kitchen-based workspace.

Why not also incorporate a place for mail, hooks for keys, a board for messages, slots for to-do paperwork, and space for newspapers and magazines? A bin for recycling paper wouldn't hurt, either. A space to charge cell phones and other gadgets will come in handy, too.

Locating the workspace smack dab next to the breakfast nook makes it easy to move from cereal and coffee to work, still in your pajamas. A waist-high wall serves to keep each function in its place.

For a workspace that's built into the kitchen cabinetry, it is a good idea to dedicate space for mail, keys, and electronic chargers. A desk incorporated into the kitchen allows family members to do a variety of tasks while staying close at hand for when it is time to eat.

This corner workspace is ideal in a multi-function space because nothing blocks the view. The cook can keep an eye on the computer, kids working at the table, and what's cooking—all at the same time.

This serene work area is truly a study-size space and is appended to the kitchen for convenience. A similar cabinetry style, color palette, and matching countertops and hardware blend the workspace seamlessly with the rest of the room.

It may be worth giving up storage space to carve out a spot for a chair like the one shown here. This spot, between a butler's pantry and the kitchen proper, offers a view to the outdoors as well as a seating area to pay bills or complete homework.

WORKSPACE SIZE

there's no reason why a workspace can't accommodate more than one person. Think about how many people will want to use the space at one time, and consider making room for at least two, so there's always a place for a parent to review a child's homework, or so that two or more people can comfortably see a slide show on the computer screen. Allow for an 18-in.- to 24-in.-deep desk-top, and fix the desk height at 26 in. for an average adult, or attach a dropped keyboard drawer. A bar-height workspace is sufficient for short work spells—and a bar stool can be pushed under the desk to free up space—but it's not ideal for a freelancer or telecommuter who spends many hours at the desk.

A library full of cookbooks is on view in this kitchen, allowing the cook to thumb through recipes by hand or on the Internet. There's room to spread out and organize paperwork, all the while keeping an eye on a cooktop that is set far enough away so heat and food spatters won't travel.

• kitchen-duty workspace

A kitchen workspace that is meant for thumbing through cookbooks or surfing the Web for recipes can be compact and close to the action. For printing out recipes for instant use, tuck a small, inexpensive printer onto a shelf below the desktop (be sure to watch out for the paper feed tray) or set up the computer for wireless printing to another household printer. Workspace can also be situated just outside the kitchen proper, which is perfect for a telecommuter who wants to work while preparing a quick meal or overseeing homework, especially with the help of a pocket door that can be pulled out to buffer sounds. For everyday tasks, such as paying bills and sorting recipes, a workspace directly in the kitchen may suit just fine. Either way, a kitchen workspace should be designed like any workspace, with consideration for proper lighting, storage, peripherals, and cable storage; but enjoy its location—close to the teakettle, coffeepot, and refrigerator.

On the flip side of this kitchen, a cook has a substantial workspace to read cookbooks, watch the news, or catch up on paperwork. Close proximity to the kitchen proper assures that a whistling teakettle or buzzing timer is within earshot.

This workspace can be closed off from the kitchen by merely pulling out the pocket door. When the door is tucked into the pocket, the rooms are completely connected. This versatility is great when it comes to large-scale entertaining or when separate spaces are desired.

cabinets

• • •

CABINETS ARE THE BACKBONE OF A KITCHEN. Their size, appearance, and construction details will influence how you choose almost every other kitchen component, from flooring to countertops to lighting. They set the style of the space and their layout determines the traffic patterns of the entire room. Given their weighty role, allow yourself plenty of time to find the cabinets that are right for you. If you decide on custom or semicustom cabinets, be prepared for a longer wait. Even stock cabinets may not be ready to pluck off the shelf at a moment's notice, so keep that in mind when you plan a renovation or building timeline. As a rule, cabinets go in before just about everything except flooring (do make sure that flooring is protected during cabinet installation). Cabinets also absorb a lion's share of any kitchen budget, so take the time to familiarize yourself with the lingo so that you can research your options effectively.

There are two main case construction techniques for cabinetry: frameless or face-frame. After deciding on the cabinet construction, think about the type of doors and drawers that fit your aesthetic and budget. Then delve into the details: cabinet materials, finishes, and hardware. The vast ocean of cabinet accessories available will allow you to organize every nook and cranny of the kitchen. Choose the door and drawer types that suit your aesthetic. There are thousands of possibilities waiting to come to life in your kitchen.

Semicustom frameless European cabinets put a fresh, clean face on this modern kitchen in New England. Deep, wide drawers fitted with heavy-duty slides support heavy pots and pans. Base cabinets have wide stainless-steel pulls, while the upper cabinets open with a gentle pull on the lower edge of the door.

face-frame or frameless

● ● ● CABINETS ALL START WITH A BOX (ALSO CALLED A CASE OR CARCASE), WHICH IS EITHER FACE-FRAME OR FRAMELESS. A face-frame cabinet, still the most common in the U.S., gets its strength and appearance from a frame of horizontal rails and vertical stiles applied to the exposed edges of the case. Doors mount onto the frame one of two ways. Inset doors fit into and flush with the frame, while overlay doors attach to the outside of the frame and sit close to the face of the frame. Because more time and care is needed to construct components that must fit closely together, face-frame cabinets with inset doors and drawers are pricier than face-frame cabinets with flush overlay doors and drawers. The least labor-intensive and, therefore, most affordable face-frame cabinets have partial overlay doors and drawers that have a wider gap between doors and drawers.

A frameless cabinet is a simple box. (Frameless cabinets are often called European cabinets because the assembly technique for these was born in Europe in the 1950s in response to a lack of lumber and the need for speedier construction.) Because there's no frame to reinforce the cabinet, the case itself must have thicker sides than a face-frame case. Doors and drawers for frameless cabinets are mounted to the case itself. Frameless cabinets are also sometimes called full-access cabinets because there's no frame to inhibit access to the inside of the case.

It's not always easy to tell face-frame cabinets from frameless, as doors and drawers for both can be flush overlay. Open a door or drawer to look at the frame. You'll see that a face-frame cabinet will have narrower drawers and pull-out shelves than a frameless cabinet, which will have the same overall width as the cabinet itself.

The beaded edges around the face-frame openings of these traditional cabinets are a painstakingly crafted detail. The doors and drawers must fit perfectly together to pull off the look.

RIGHT These tall frameless cabinets with full overlay doors provide ample pantry storage. Everyday items are close at hand in the tall lower cabinets and seasonal gear is stowed behind the flip-top doors of the top cabinets.

FAR RIGHT No need to add hardware to these frameless semicustom European cabinets: The reveal overlay drawers are easily opened with fingertips. Stainless-steel trim makes the cabinet edges durable and easy to clean.

These frameless case cabinets have a modern case style but take on a traditional appearance thanks to hefty vintage-style bin pulls and frame-and-flat-panel doors and drawers.

more about...
CABINET TYPES

- Doors and drawers overlay the case completely.

- Concealed adjustable hinges on frameless cabinets are easily adjusted over the lifetime of the cabinet.

- Fixed or adjustable shelves are a less-expensive option in both frameless and face-frame cabinets, but pullout shelves allow complete access to contents.

- Doors and drawers can be inset (traditional) or can overlay the frame fully (flush overlay) or partially (reveal overlay).

- Traditional inset door hinges on face-frame cabinets are visible when the door is closed; concealed adjustable hinges are an available alternative. Flush overlay doors must have concealed hinges, while reveal overlay doors can have either type.

- The face frame strengthens the cabinet case.

- The face frame reduces a cabinet's opening size, so drawers and pullout shelves are narrower than in a frameless cabinet with the same width.

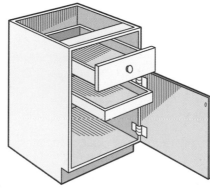

Frameless cabinet

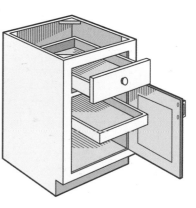

Face-frame cabinet

configuring cabinets

● ● ● THE LAYOUT OF CABINETS DIRECTS THE FLOW OF TRAFFIC IN THE KITCHEN. The floor plans determine this configuration, but consider how cabinets fit vertically as well. Study elevations to make sure that the cabinets are situated well and easy to use. The standard base cabinet is just shy of 2 ft. deep and usually 34½ in. tall to allow for a 1½-in.-thick countertop (including the substrate layer) for a countertop height of 36 in. total. For a 30-in.-deep countertop, install cabinets 4 in. to 5 in. away from the wall and make sure that the ends are covered with a panel wide enough to cover the gap. Think about specifying taller base cabinets, or set a standard case on a tall toekick for tall cooks.

Stock wall cabinets are usually 12 in. deep and 30 in. high. If set at the preferred 18 in. above a standard 36-in.-high countertop, they won't reach the ceiling, so consider adding decorative storage or lighting in this uppermost area. You can also install stock wall cabinets so that they touch the ceiling, but remember that upper shelves will be harder to reach. You may need wall cabinets deeper than 12 in. to accommodate large dinner plates and chargers. It could be that only an extra ½ in. is necessary inside. If you decide to spring for extra-deep wall cabinets, you'll want a deeper countertop if you use the counter for workspace. If a microwave oven is going into a wall cabinet, take note that most models are deeper than 12 in. Especially deep wall cabinets—15 in. or more—can be dropped to countertop height to give a china-cabinet effect and offer dish storage at a comfortable height.

BELOW, LEFT
Different styles of cabinets look dynamic in the same kitchen if they share a few common characteristics. These face-frame stained cabinets with raised inset frame-and-panel doors pair well with the painted island cabinets, which have flat panels.

BELOW, RIGHT
These custom-made face-frame cabinets feature reveal overlay doors and drawers. Wall cabinets hold dishes, while the tall cabinets provide pantry space.

RIGHT Taking advantage of every inch of space, this urban kitchen's frameless cabinets stretch to the ceiling, creating a narrow reveal—a smart detail for when a ceiling isn't perfectly level.

BELOW Fitted with frame-and-panel doors and drawers, these cabinets feature a toekick along the bottom for a comfortable workspace, which contrasts nicely with the wider base of the floor-to-ceiling pantry stack.

Dishwasher and wine cooler fit neatly behind the frame-and-panel full overlay doors of these frameless cabinets. A thick panel above the wall cabinets contains inset task lighting and recessed fixtures that shine upward to illuminate the ceiling.

In this large traditional kitchen, wall cabinets meet the ceiling with crown molding trimming the joint. Lighting within and under the cabinets transforms this storage area into a space for displaying family heirlooms alongside everyday dishware.

• space above cabinets

What goes inside a cabinet is only the beginning of your storage options. Use extra space above standard-height wall cabinets for display; tuck lighting behind cornices to add ambience; or drop the ceiling to make a soffit for lighting or ductwork. For taller wall cabinets, make sure doors clear light fixtures and double-check that sufficient space remains for trim to fit between the top of the door and ceiling; an elaborate cornice requires more space, of course. While trim eases the visual and physical transition between cabinet and ceiling, many trimless contemporary-style cabinets are flush with the ceiling or set off by a narrow reveal. Both details demand an exceptionally flat ceiling for good effect.

The semicustom cabinets are a built-in feature of this kitchen. Narrow soffits top the wall cabinets in the corner of the room and the two tall pantries tuck into framed drywall niches.

Here's a good-looking way to deal with the transition space between cabinets and ceiling: A band of trim stained to match the cabinets fits snugly against the dropped ceiling of the niche.

SPACE BENEATH CABINETS

@ toespace is made with a separate, recessed platform that supports the cabinet from below or by a piece of trim that conceals support legs. Stock face-frame and manufactured frameless cabinets typically have 4-in.-high, 3-in.-deep toespaces. European-style cabinetry usually has taller toespaces (5 in. to 8 in. high), making it easier to clean the floor without damaging the cabinets. The higher rise also elevates the contents of the cabinet for easier access. Toespaces are handy for storing step stools or the family silver, or can house heat and return-air registers.

One of the hallmarks of unfitted cabinetry is a toespace adorned with legs to look like furniture. There's generally a dark-colored recessed panel, curved or straight depending on the style, set about 3 in. behind the legs. Some island cabinets are designed to rest on plinths that project from the case; working comfortably at this kind of island will require a deeper countertop so that there is room for the cook's feet.

Cabinet bottoms follow both ergonomics and style, with a recessed sink cabinet and toespace deep enough for standing comfortably. In contrast, the flanking cabinets rest on a plinth with baseboard.

doors and drawers

● ● ● AFTER CHOOSING THE RIGHT KIND OF CABINET FOR YOUR KITCHEN, TURN YOUR ATTENTION TO DOORS AND DRAWERS. Inset doors and drawers sit flush within a cabinet's face frame. They are certainly an age-old standard, but nowadays cost more than overlay doors and drawers because of the precision required to build them. The traditional hinge used on an inset door is a butt hinge, usually finished to match pulls and knobs.

Overlay doors and drawers are affixed to the surface of a face-frame case or the interior of a frameless case. Adjustable cup hinges allow doors to be easily realigned or repositioned. Full overlay doors and drawers are always the standard on frameless cabinets and very often are used on face-frame cabinets as well. The door rests just a hair's breadth away from the drawer, which means it takes more care to build and install them than reveal overlay doors and drawers, which are spaced farther apart. Reveal overlay doors (also called partial overlay) are used on face-frame cabinets. Reveal overlay doors and drawers don't require quite as much alignment and precision, so labor costs will be less than those for full overlay doors.

Flat, one-piece drawers pair nicely with frame-and-panel cabinet doors, whether painted or in natural wood—both looks are found in this kitchen. Pulls are sized to match, with small pulls on drawers and slightly wider pulls on base cabinet doors.

FACING PAGE Inset drawers and doors give this kitchen a traditional look, as do the furniture feet. The variety of hardware spices up the space, with pulls for narrow drawers near the range and knobs on storage drawers and doors.

ABOVE The locally crafted custom cabinets in this kitchen are made from sapele, a sustainable exotic wood similar to mahogany. Full overlay doors and drawers in frameless cases are finished with modern metal pulls, a nice contrast to the warm color of the wood.

Inset drawers are often set into individual frames in a face-frame case, but to optimize space it makes sense to stack drawers within one frame, as seen here. The upper one-piece drawers are set into individual frames for contrast.

Full overlay doors and a wide top drawer make full use of this cabinet space and offer surface area to feature luxurious figured wood. Patterned glass offers an impressionist view of the cabinet's contents.

Storage options in the wall cabinets of this kitchen are visually differentiated. Everyday dishware resides in the larger, lower wood cabinets. Less frequently used items are displayed in the upper cabinets, where glass doors make it easy to spot what is stored.

In this modern kitchen, high-tech hardware adds to the industrial-chic look and allows cabinet doors to lift up and out of the way with a slight tug on the pull.

With full overlay glass-panel doors sans pulls, these wall cabinets pair nicely with the neutral base cabinets and show off a bright and colorful collection of dishes.

DOOR OPTIONS

Cabinet doors provide a continuous surface for detailing, so here's where raised panels, beadboard panels, textured glass, and carving can take center stage. Glass panels in frame-and-panel doors are a great, affordable way to show off stored dishes. Glazed panels tend to cost more than wood, so if the budget needs tightening, install glass doors on a selection of cabinets to get the most

visual impact. Of course, cabinets with clear glass doors can showcase a good many items, so take the time to consider how you want to make use of this display space. See the gallery of door options on p. 87.

Patterned or frosted glass gives cabinets an openness similar to fully transparent glass, but allows for a diffused view of a cabinet's interior. For extra sparkle, add recessed or

surface-mounted puck lights or rope lights to the top interior of glass-paneled cabinets. To keep door sizes small but storage options wide open, add a row of cabinets above standard-size wall cabinets. Doors on these upper cabinets can flip up or swing open, and provide another place for some added style with decorative knobs or accent panels.

Doors and drawers can vary harmoniously, as in this traditional kitchen, where face-frame cabinets fitted with inset one-piece drawers are a nice counterpoint to the deeper frame-and-panel drawers underneath the countertop.

• types of doors and drawers

Whether they are inset or overlay, doors and drawers come in two basic types. Frame-and-panel doors are the more traditional type. The frame is usually solid wood, and the panels are solid as well or made of veneered medium-density fiberboard (MDF). Panels can be flat, beaded, beveled, perforated, carved wood (or woodlike material), or glass—clear or patterned.

Flat-slab (also called one-piece) doors and drawers are made from glued solid wood or

MDF that is veneered with any number of materials, including wood, plastic laminate, metal, or glass. All-metal doors and drawers are available, too, and since they are not made from chemicals that can outgas, they have a certain green appeal. Don't feel obliged to match every drawer and door in your kitchen. A flat-panel drawer above frame-and-panel doors makes a pleasing balance, and contrasting materials and colors can add high style.

Cabinet doors are available in two basic types: flat slab or frame and panel. Flat-slab doors can look contemporary or take on a traditional look with applied moldings. The style of frame-and-panel doors depends mostly on the panel design and material. Both door types can be used in frameless or face-frame cases.

door types: frame-and-panel doors

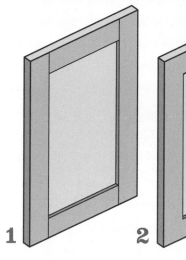
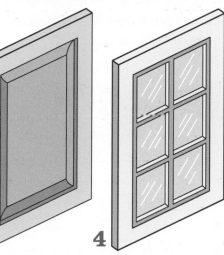
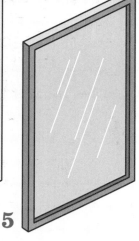

1 **2** **3** **4** **5**

1 A frame-and-panel door is made up of vertical stiles and horizontal rails with a panel between them.

2 The panel can be flat and made of any material, such as beadboard, shown here.

3 Beading is applied to the frame, an easier job than applying beading to the face frame itself. The raised panel can be solid wood or a panel product.

4 Single or divided-lite glazing displays cabinet contents. Align interior shelves with seams of the glass doors for a tidy look.

5 Thin metal frame with a translucent glass or acrylic panel

frameless doors

6 **7** **8**

6 A flat-slab (or one-piece) door can be made of any kind of veneered or coated-panel product, plastic, or metal. Solid wood makes a relatively unstable one-piece door.

7 Flat-slab door with edge-glued solid wood or veneered pieces

8 Flat-slab door with applied molding to simulate a frame-and-panel door

The no-nonsense, streamlined look of this bank of cabinets hides major storage options inside. A deep drawer opens to reveal a shallow knife and utensil drawer that fits neatly over stacks of dishes.

This skillfully crafted silverware drawer with dovetailed corners allows silver to be stored upright and retrieved quickly. Interiors lined with felt, and a walnut trim, provide functional and elegant detailing.

It's easier to lift dishes from a drawer than reach into a base cabinet to retrieve them. An extra-wide drawer beside the range provides convenience when it's time to plate dinner and allows fixed cabinet shelves to be used for other storage.

•drawer options

Drawers store so many items in the kitchen, so you want ones that will stand the test of time. The strongest, prettiest drawers have dovetailed corners. Drawers with corners that are doweled, screwed, or stapled are less expensive, but if built well can do the job. Heavy-duty drawers are made of ⅝-in. to ¾-in. sides of melamine, solid wood, or birch plywood, while shallow or narrow drawers may have sides as thin as ½ in. Don't rule out plastic or metal drawer sides. They can be plenty strong and enhance contemporary cabinets with their streamlined look.

•drawer slides

Full-extension slides allow access to the entire length of a drawer. That convenience may convince you to pay the extra expense, if only for slides on big drawers that house pots and pans and on shallow drawers that hold aluminum foil and plastic wrap or flatware. Quiet, self-closing slides are an added feature that you may be willing to spring for, especially in a house of enthusiastic door and drawer slammers. If a traditional look is important—or if you don't like the look of side-mounted slides—consider undermount slides, but keep in mind that these cost more than side-mounted. Undermount slides reduce the depth of the drawer, but side-mounted slides shave off a bit of width. In any case, make sure slides are sized to support the weight of a drawer and its expected contents

ABOVE A narrow dish drawer rides on partially hidden undermount slides. Its location next to the dishwasher makes putting away clean dishes a quick chore and setting the table a matter of just a few steps.

TOP LEFT These spice and pot drawers have hidden, undermount slides, which keep the drawer sides neat but make the drawers a little shallower. The warming drawer at left has an identical drawer front and, when closed, conceals the appliance.

BOTTOM LEFT A dish drawer like this one requires heavy-duty slides for support. This drawer is at the perfect height for children and adults to access, and it is within easy reach of the dishwasher.

Wire shelves pull out for
complete visibility. When closed,
the sliding glass doors keep
dishes from getting dusty,
and when opened, they don't
encroach on the workspace.

• pullout shelves

An alternative to fixed shelves or base cabinet drawers is pullout shelves. Pullout shelves are similar to drawers, but they have lower sides and fronts. The sides and fronts can be solid, but also consider glass, Plexiglas®, or wire for better visibility. Wire shelves allow for ventilation, which comes in handy when storing pantry items. Pullouts store all kinds of kitchen gear—cans and jars, spices, pots and pans, pot lids, trays, and baking sheets. For added organization, fit them with built-in dividers or after-market accessories.

LEFT Most sliding shelves are shallow, but this deep one—call it a pullout drawer—is ideal for storing pot lids and small cutting boards on their sides. The fixed shelf above works for storing larger trays and pans.

ABOVE TOP Stacked sliding shelves support the weight of large pots and pans. Adjacent to the range, this cabinet spot makes an ideal location for storing heavy cookware.

ABOVE BOTTOM Wire pullout shelving allows the cook to see where items are at a glance, even on lower levels. Another plus is that wire allows air circulation, which makes a difference when storing vegetables like potatoes and onions.

drawer storage

SIZES. Drawers are a different story. When stowing items in drawers, pay close attention to the size and configuration of the items so that none of the contents snag when next you open the drawer. Oversized food-wrap boxes may not fit in standard stock cabinetry drawers.

Deep drawers for pots and pans are best left undivided, while deep drawers for plate storage should have dowels or flat dividers installed to prevent collisions. Think about adding trays, slots, or dividers to shallow drawers to keep small tools organized. Consider whether it's more convenient to store spices inclined in slanted trays or standing in a deeper drawer with labeled jar tops. To get the drawer storage you need at the price you want, it may be worthwhile to compare the cost of after-market accessories to the cost of the accessories included in your cabinet order.

The inside of this drawer is as sleek and organized as the outside. All the contents are visible thanks to the stainless-steel cutlery dividers, and there is a narrow column of space on the end for longer items or dishtowels.

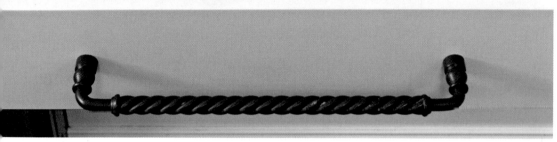

ABOVE A place for every cooking utensil is what this drawer provides. Accessories are organized by type, and adjustable section dividers change the size of the metal trays with a quick snap.

BELOW The silverware drawer has built-in sections to keep cutlery from getting mixed up. The neighboring knife drawer holds larger utensils and a pullout cutting board. It has an indented lip in place of a pull or knob.

ABOVE TOP A deep drawer with shelves that tilt slightly makes an ideal space to store all your spices. This drawer is adjacent to the range, so seasonings are just an arm's length away from where the cooking takes place.

ABOVE BOTTOM A knife drawer alleviates the need for a knife block to occupy space on the countertop. This custom-made slotted wood insert keeps knives clean, secure, and ready to use.

Ideal for a baker with limited counter space, this cabinet has a swing-out door that opens to reveal an appliance nook housing a mixer and baking tools.

Behind closed doors these cabinets look run-of-the-mill. But the addition of swivel-hinged shelves turns this tight space into a multi-layered pantry with plenty of storage possibilities.

SPECIALIZED CABINETRY

think about having a few cabinets in the kitchen that will perform specific functions. Start by setting aside space for specialized storage, such as for large, flat items like trays, baking sheets, and cutting boards. You can store these vertically or horizontally, depending on your preference. Narrow vertical slots make accessing these items easier than horizontal storage, as there's no need to sort through stacks. Roll-outs—those tall, multilevel storage accessories—can hold cleaning supplies, pantry items, workspace gadgets, cutlery, spices, oils, and vinegars.

Cabinetry designed specifically for pullout garbage and recycling bins is a great option, but consider your cooking habits. If two people work in the kitchen, the cabinet under the sink is the least convenient place to put the trash. Instead, think about storing garbage and composting bins near food-prep areas. A pedal-operated trash cabinet slides out to allow the cook to dump trimmings without touching the handle with dirty hands; an alternative is a trash cabinet that can be eased out with a foot. For recycling cans and bottles, consider storing a bin within reach of the sink.

ABOVE An easy reach from the sink, this trash cabinet makes it easy to scrape off plates before they go in the dishwasher. The second container could be used as an additional garbage bag, compost container, or recycling bin.

LEFT Where countertop space is limited, a food processor finds a handy home on a lift-up shelf, close to an electrical receptacle. A narrow pullout drawer houses spices.

This full-length pullout unit looks like two cabinets from the outside. It opens to reveal shelves and a metal rack with snap-on attachments to hold utensils and cleaning supplies and to provide miscellaneous storage for the kitchen workspace.

RIGHT This appliance cupboard with pull-down door slides keeps items dust free and out of the way when not in use. But when needed, the appliances are merely pulled out and plugged into the outlets conveniently located within the cupboard.

FAR RIGHT This shallow niche covered with a mini-garage door houses cooking utensils and is an unobtrusive home to receptacles, handy for plugging in an immersion blender or hand mixer.

Narrow space is used to good advantage in this kitchen. Accessories like these pullout mesh rack storage systems keep the area around the sink uncluttered: Pegs, hooks, and shelves store brushes, soaps, and cleaning gear.

97

This wire rack accessory is a space-saver's dream. The rack swivels as it turns, and its four shelves transform the hard-to-reach interior of a blind corner cabinet into no-fuss storage.

• cabinet corners

There are a number of creative solutions for making use of blind cabinet corners—those hard-to-reach recesses created when two runs of cabinets intersect at a right angle. Keep an eye out for a lazy Susan without a center post for more flexible storage or one with wire shelves for better visibility. Complex swing-out and pullout racks allow access to the entire storage space, but do remember that the more moving parts, the higher the cost. As you contemplate corner cabinets,

always make sure that there's room for doors and drawers to open fully.

Wall cabinets have corners, too, but they aren't usually as hard to access because of their shallow depth. But if wall corner cabinets are stumping you, try fitting them with well-lit, open shelving. It solves access problems and makes a kitchen seem more spacious, and you have added places for displaying family photos or prized possessions.

BELOW There is no blind corner in this wall cabinet, as the two cabinets join to make an L-shaped storage space. The right-hand two-leaf door is double hinged to fold back on itself.

RIGHT Heavy-duty, kidney-shaped shelves may look unconventional, but they are designed specifically for blind corner cabinets.

A lazy Susan made from wire makes every inch of this lower corner cabinet visible and accessible. Finishing the cabinet interior in white makes it even easier to see.

hardware

●●● HARDWARE IS PHYSICALLY A SMALL PART OF THE KITCHEN-CABINET PACKAGE, BUT IT HAS A BIG IMPACT ON PERCEIVED QUALITY, so spending a little more for style and functionality is well worth it. Think about splurging on hidden hardware, particularly drawer slides and hinges. Full-extension, soft-closing slides are pricey, but are worth it in terms of convenience. Visible hardware—knobs, pulls, and butt hinges—varies in cost depending on finish and source, with one-of-a-kind artisan pieces costing far more than manufactured hardware.

Of course you will want to match knobs, pulls, and hinges to fit your kitchen's aesthetic. But the trick to getting hardware that all looks great together is to establish a common denominator, such as a finish, and then to use different sizes and shapes. You can also use the same-shaped hardware, but vary the finish. Changing the hardware on a stand-alone run of cabinets (and giving cabinets a different finish) can add to the unfitted-kitchen look.

FAR LEFT These cool, translucent cabinets are faced with mirrored glass and fitted with bold stainless-steel pulls on both doors and drawers.

LEFT Simple metal tab pulls atop these doors and drawers give an uncluttered look to a cheerful, modern kitchen.

FACING PAGE The simple elegance of these Shaker-style doors with wide stiles is heightened by the polished, oval-shaped nickel doorknobs and drawer pulls.

• knobs and pulls

As a matter of proportion, knobs usually go on drawers and pulls are found on cabinet doors. But this isn't a hard-and-fast rule. Knobs and pulls can look great on either drawers or doors. Just keep proportion in mind—a 1¼-in. knob is a comfortable size for standard-size drawers. A bigger knob or bin pull can look awkward on the face of a small drawer. Drawers over 24 in. usually require a long pull, or two pulls or knobs—remember to use two to prevent the drawer from eventually racking.

A knob with a rose (a round plate at the base of the shaft) helps keep fingernails from scratching the drawer or door finish. Bin pulls stay shinier longer because fingers grasp them along the inner side of the pull. But these can also be a little tougher to clean than knobs or wire pulls.

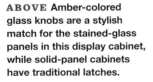

ABOVE Amber-colored glass knobs are a stylish match for the stained-glass panels in this display cabinet, while solid-panel cabinets have traditional latches.

RIGHT The small size and simple line of these cabinet knobs are purposefully unobtrusive, so that the warm tones of the maple panels and frames attract the eye.

These antique bronze pulls are just the right size for these face-frame cabinet drawers. Anything larger would be too heavy for the cabinet design, but a smaller pull would seem insubstantial.

Low-profile wood button knobs keep the character of this large kitchen island understated and traditional.

ABOVE Adjustable and concealed cup hinges on wall cabinets like this one allow doors to be adjusted and readjusted without difficulty.

LEFT The lone beaded-edge frame-and-panel door is an anomaly in this sea of drawers. Concealed hinges were used instead of the more traditional exposed butt hinge to give the door a smoother look.

• hinges

Concealed adjustable hinges are standard for frameless cabinets. Unlike butt hinges, adjustable hinges allow cabinet doors to be realigned with ease. Concealed adjustable hinges also allow cabinets to open roughly 180 degrees, so when doors are ajar they don't jut out into space. If you are a family prone to slamming doors, look into adjustable hinges with a built-in soft-closing feature. Adjustable hinges are available for inset doors in face frame cabinets as well; these can't open a full 180 degrees but allow skewed or crooked doors to be realigned without fuss.

The more traditional hinges for inset doors are butt hinges, either non-mortised or mortised. Installing mortised butt hinges requires extra time and precision but creates a smooth fit along the door and frame.

If cabinet hinges aren't self-closing, you may want to add catches to keep doors closed. Catches range from mechanical devices that hook together to invisible rare-earth magnets, which can be inserted into door and stile or case to hold the door shut. Latches are traditional closers that give an antique look, but they take more effort to open and close.

TOP RIGHT Nickel ball-end butt hinges and pulls of matching nickel are elegant and subtle hardware choices for traditional inset doors.

BOTTOM RIGHT Crisp accents, these black twisted wire pulls match the knobs and butt hinges of the traditional, white-painted cabinets.

materials and finishes

● ● ● CABINET INTERIORS DO THE HEAVY LIFTING FOR CABINETRY, but the materials and finishes you choose for cabinet exteriors will contribute largely to your kitchen's style. Most cabinets are wood, whether solid or veneered onto cabinet cases, doors, and drawers. Many manufacturers and cabinet shops offer an exciting array of wood species and finishes, so you are sure to find one that pleases. If historic style is a factor, think quartersawn oak, cherry, Douglas fir, pine, hickory, chestnut, or maple. These species can also look great with modern detailing and treatment. Less-traditional species like sapele, bamboo, and zebrawood are usually reserved for contemporary cabinets.

Most wood cabinets are sprayed with catalyzed varnish, but for a timeworn patina consider investing in hand-applied finishes, though these will come at a considerably higher cost. Hand-applied glazes and paints and high-gloss lacquer are the most costly finishes. Paint may be just the thing to dress up cabinets built from medium-density fiberboard or wood that's not stain-grade. But painted cabinets—especially those with glossy finishes—will show wear and tear more than clear-finished wood cabinets, and may not be as easy to touch up. Door- and drawer-panel products (plywood or MDF) can be veneered with wood, rigid thermofoil (RTF), metal, or not-your-mom's plastic laminate. Stainless-steel and coated steel cabinets are also fashionable, with their pro-style gleam and durability.

The veneered wood and panels in this kitchen make a lively pattern of horizontals and verticals as they stretch across the length of the base cabinets.

The kitchen island is a unique element by virtue of its location, and highlighting it with contrasting colors or materials makes good design sense. This dark wood–faced island with butcher-block countertop stands out against the cream-colored, marble-topped cabinets in the rest of the kitchen.

Light green stain gives a refreshing look to these streamlined frameless wall cabinets, while the dark brown base cabinets act as a rich backdrop. Matching brown tab pulls blend with the base cabinets for a unified look.

A multilayered decorative paint finish creates an antique patina on the doors and cases of these cabinets, appropriate for a traditional country kitchen.

• material choices

What lies beneath your cabinetry's gorgeous doors and drawers may not seem exciting, but take note of what your cabinet cases will be made from. Higher-quality cases of ¾-in. plywood last longer than medium-density fiberboard and particleboard, and hold fasteners better. They will also support heavy countertops without buckling or sagging, and they are more resistant to moisture than medium-density fiberboard (MDF) and particleboard. Some cabinetmakers, however, prefer MDF more than plywood because of its dimensional stability and smooth face,

which is ideal for applying veneers and other laminates.

Case interiors can be painted, veneered with plastic laminate or wood (maple and beech are popular choices), or finished more economically with vinyl, foil, or paper films. Melamine that is thermofused onto particleboard makes a case with a ready-made, easy-to-clean surface. It comes in white or black, or can be patterned to look like wood. Melamine is a sound option because it is more affordable than wood veneer and outlasts paint or film.

Cabinets with melamine-faced particleboard cases and doors and drawers faced in stainless steel give this kitchen a clean, modern style. Neither pulls nor knobs disrupt the streamlined look, as doors and drawers open by magnetic touch latch.

COST CONSIDERATIONS

t he more complex the cabinet design, the higher the cost. Multiaction, swing-out shelves cost more than pullout shelves. Frame-and-panel doors are pricier than flat-panel doors and drawers of the same construction quality. Raised panels cost more than flat panels. Corners are expensive to build and assemble, so a straight run of cabinets that fits between walls (eliminating the need for end panels) costs less than an L-shaped run of cabinets that doesn't abut walls. But that's not always the case, as a straight run of cabinetry that's 8 ft. tall with ornate detailing can easily cost more than a U-shaped configuration that's standard in height and simple in detail.

So that you don't get sticker shock along the way, keep in mind that certain cabinetry features come with higher prices. Cabinets with custom widths and heights, plywood cases, frame-and-panel doors, inset doors and drawers, glazes and other multistep finishes, butt hinges, full extension slides, and complex accessories cost more. Here are a few thrifty options to consider: particleboard cases, paint-grade doors and drawers, 1/4-in. drawer bottoms, lip pulls instead of applied knobs or pulls, and buying after-market accessories. But don't just think about initial savings. If you plan to keep your kitchen cabinets for a long time, paying up front for higher-quality cabinets may be the way to go.

ABOVE These full overlay birch-plywood cabinet doors are finished with mirrored translucent glass, which gives a luminous shimmer to this kitchen's storage spaces.

LEFT These wall cabinet doors have wide interior frames covered by translucent glass. Both are set into a thin stainless-steel frame and fitted with long handles.

stock cabinets

● ● ● THERE'S NO ONE SOURCE FOR STOCK CABINETRY. They can be bought off the shelf or ordered from a big-box store, home center, or lumberyard. You can also purchase them through a kitchen products dealer, designer, or contractor. As a general rule, stock cabinets are built as individual components in standard sizes and 3-in. increments (i.e., cabinets are 12-, 15-, 18-in. wide and so on), so if a run of cabinets isn't quite as wide as the space for them, filler pieces can span the gaps. For a more custom look, cover gaps, embellish corners, and augment the tops of wall cabinets with cornices purchased from decorative-molding suppliers. Stock cabinets come in a dizzying variety of finishes, colors, styles, and sizes, and they still tend to cost about half the price of many semicustom or custom cabinets.

Off-the-shelf stock cabinets are available in modern and traditional styles. These streamlined cabinets are high-gloss red laminate with stainless-steel pulls and a faux stainless-steel toekick that is actually plastic laminate.

These American-made semicustom cabinets deliver stylish contrast: The raised-panel cherry doors on the island and in the mudroom look sharp against the white laminate flat-panel doors and single-piece drawers of the perimeter cabinets.

• semicustom cabinets

Semicustom manufacturers are similar to stock manufacturers in that both build their wares in factories rather than small shops. Semicustom offerings, however, tend to be of a higher quality, with a wider range of styles, finishes, hardware, accessories, sizes, and configurations available. They can also supply longer stretches of cabinets and a wider range of configurations. Typically, semicustom cabinets also offer a range of custom-level detailing, such as dovetailed drawers.

RIGHT Semicustom European cabinets with an easy-care, high-gloss acrylic laminate are a functional and stylish choice for this modern kitchen. Stainless-steel pulls match the backsplash, countertops, and oven.

•custom cabinets

Depending on the shop, custom cabinets aren't necessarily the most expensive option for cabinetry, but they tend to be. Their fabrication also often takes longer than semicustom cabinets. Custom cabinets aren't always built from scratch, and a cabinetmaker can cut down on the time it takes to deliver your order without compromising quality by installing components from several specialized sources into shop-built cases. If the components are well made, this way of cabinetmaking delivers a high-quality product with a much shorter lead time.

No matter the cabinet source you choose, take time to study carefully the plans, shop drawings, and specifications available. As with any custom-made product, ask for references and make sure to take a glance at their work in person. Also, get to know the hardware, accessories, and cabinet components that you can pick from.

all about...
DO-IT-YOURSELF CABINETS

knocked-down (KD) or ready-to-assemble (RTA) cabinets are factory-manufactured and -finished cabinet components that ship to you with all the necessary parts, fasteners, and instructions included. Holes are predrilled and sometimes dowels are preglued. The intent is that no specialized power tools are required for assembling the cabinets, making them a viable and affordable option for anyone who's fairly handy and patient.

IKEA® is the KD and RTA company that everyone's heard of, but there are smaller companies out there, so be sure to search for both KD and RTA sources online. The term "RTA" sometimes applies to cabinet components that are sold exclusively to the trade or to serious amateur woodworkers who can speak the lingo. Find a provider who sells directly to homeowners or become familiar with the terminology, or hire a craftsperson to give you a hand. With careful research, design, planning, and follow-through, an intrepid homeowner may even mix and match KD/RTA options—ordering cabinet components from one company and doors and drawers from another.

Ready-to-assemble, off-the-shelf cabinets like these offer relatively inexpensive yet stylish storage options. Details like translucent glass doors that hinge or flip and drawers with recessed finger pulls make the cabinets look one-of-a-kind.

A local cabinetmaker built these frameless cabinets with full overlay sapele-veneer doors and drawers for this North Carolina kitchen.

open shelves & pantries

• • •

CABINETS MAY BE THE REPOSITORIES OF MOST KITCHEN GEAR, BUT THERE'S MUCH TO BE SAID ABOUT THE BENEFITS OF OPEN SHELVING, whether it is out in the open or behind a closed door in a pantry. Like items can be conveniently clustered together. A quick glance lets you verify that supplies are at the ready in advance of a snowstorm or pack of hungry teenagers. Collections of beloved dishes or antique spice jars can be displayed side by side with stacks of plates and rows of home-canned preserves. Open shelves showcase decorative objects and everyday kitchen items, keeping them both visible and easy to find at a moment's notice. Open storage is also great for those large, awkward items that you want at hand but that don't fit in a cabinet.

But what if you prefer keeping some things out of sight but not out of mind? This is where the pantry fits in, and why it's come out of retirement. A pantry is well worth the space it monopolizes in the kitchen, whether built into kitchen cabinetry or surrounded by three walls and a door. Open shelving in a pantry offers the same easy access and ability to see instantly what you need to restock on your next trip to the grocery store. But pantries don't have to be fancy or as organized as open shelving because they aren't on view. Except for the butler's pantry, of course; as the traditional transition between kitchen and dining room, it is often more elegant than the kitchen itself.

Fixed shelves look more traditional than adjustable shelves, suitable for a kitchen with a rustic, country-style aesthetic.

open shelves

●●● OPEN SHELVES CAN GO ANYWHERE AND BE OF ANY SIZE. Tuck skinny shelves in a recess between studs or between the top of the backsplash and the bottom of wall cabinets. These shelves are great for stowing spices, tea, and small jars holding teaspoons and other small tools. Fit open shelves between runs of closed cabinets, particularly at corners, or at the end of a run of cabinets to make a small kitchen seem more spacious. Position open shelves over workspaces for a comfortable reach; shelves that are lower than 16 in. to 18 in. above the countertop should be no deeper than 12 in. Like wall cabinets, the bottom front edge of open shelves can conceal task lighting.

ABOVE The dishes on these shelves, supported by hidden brackets, receive light from all angles: A flanking window gives natural light and puck lights built into the hollow wood shelves illuminate from above.

LEFT Open shelves add character and convenience to a kitchen and are ideal for displaying decorative dishes or much-used items. Even neat stacks of plates and cups can transcend mere inventory to become objects of art. These shelves are open on the side to capture light.

LEFT Mixing and matching open shelves with closed cabinets like those in this retro-style kitchen offers the best of both worlds: places to display heirlooms or keep cookbooks alongside shelves that are hidden from view.

BELOW These baskets, hung from sliding wood brackets, blur the line between drawers and open shelving. Baskets provide stylish ventilation for fresh breads and are a good place to stow kids' snacks.

LEFT Beaded face-frame cabinets without doors offer several different places to use paint, making intricately colored display cases for kitchen objects.

• shelving materials

Aesthetics and budget play a big role in what materials you decide to use for shelving. Solid wood and woodlike panel products look traditional or modern depending on the finish, while wire shelves give ventilation, visibility, and the look of a streamlined restaurant kitchen.

Delicate in appearance, glass shelves maximize available light and are useful for displaying items. Structural support for shelving can be minimal or decorative, such as oversized arts and crafts brackets, depending on your personal taste.

ABOVE Open shelving of various sizes contrasts nicely with the closed storage in this kitchen, and the dark-stained door panels create a complex pattern. The lower shelves are fitted with receptacles for appliances.

This pantry, made from semicustom European cabinets, occupies a prominent place between the kitchen and family room. Pullout shelves are installed in the entire unit except for the bottom center shelf, which stores pans and trays in vertical slots.

all about...
SHELF DEPTH

S helves come in any size or configuration that you could need or want, but it's helpful to consider a few guidelines for shelf depth. For cookbooks, make sure the shelf is 8 in. to 12 in. deep. It is a good idea to store dishware on shelves that are 8 in. to 15 in. deep. Big, bulky items like roasting pans and small appliances should fit on 10-in.- to 18-in.-deep shelves. To avoid stacking items sky-high, make sure shelves are built close together or in pairs or trios. That makes dishes or cookware easier to retrieve.

This thin stretch of wood shelves extends the whole length of the countertop and range. Stained a rich brown to match the island top, the spice shelf adds color and depth to a white kitchen.

Open shelves eliminate awkward corners, as seen in this handsome set of profiled solid wood shelves supported by elaborate wood cleats and brackets. Narrow shelves turn the corner and provide space for hanging cups.

pantries

● ● ● WHAT MAKES A PANTRY? SHELVES, AND LOTS OF THEM. That definition, however, doesn't begin to cover the range of configurations and layouts that pantries can take. Cabinet-style pantries come in a variety of styles. A base cabinet pantry with stacks of pullout shelves behind a door is one option. A slender, 7-ft.-tall rollout cabinet with stacks of fixed shelves is another choice for easy-access storage. And there is always a multilayered swing-out pantry. Many cabinet and hardware manufacturers offer highly complex—and pricey—storage systems with shelves that swivel in and out, somewhat like a revolving door.

The pantry that's a room in itself can either be a closet-size space that you reach into or a full-blown walk-in room. If it is the latter, sometimes the space is big enough for a workspace, bar, or laundry. The benefit of pantry closets and walk-in pantries is that everything is in sight. There are no shelves to pull out or flip up. Every inch of a pantry can be covered with narrow shelves or hooks and racks. The ideal pantry location is in a cool spot, clear of the range and other heat sources.

BELOW Shelves in this pantry vary in depth and materials. Closely spaced fixed shelves handle the heaviest, bulkiest items. There's room for a microwave to hang over the abbreviated countertop as well.

When closed, this pullout pantry in a modern kitchen is disguised to look like three small cabinets. Metal racks spaced at varying heights allow for flexible storage.

This pantry is packed. Spacious rotating metal shelves in the center and adjustable shelves on the doors make it convenient to store everything from small spice jars to large, bulky items. Recessed halogen puck lights turn on when the doors open.

LEFT The bulk of food storage in this kitchen is handled by the built-in pantry with adjustable roll-out shelves. Baskets and boxes corral smaller items.

BELOW A bright green wall covered in crisp white beadboard provides a backdrop for the cans and jars on these narrow Plexiglas shelves. A bar with hooks for objects with handles takes up the last bit of open space below.

PANTRY SHELVES

*a*djustable shelves or free-standing shelving kits make it easy to adapt the storage of your pantry over the years. If, however, you know what you want and where, fixed shelves are fine, especially if you like a more traditional look. Solid shelves look traditional, while wire shelves offer better visibility and ventilation. Baskets add warmth and visual interest to a pantry. They work well for corralling small items—potatoes, onions, bags of snacks, kids' toys—and are easy to take out and put back.

A countertop in the pantry offers additional storage and is a place to tuck small appliances or cool (or hide) just-baked cookies. A stack of skinny, deep shelves can hold large, flat items such as baking pans, trays, or sheets of parchment paper.

Good lighting is essential in the pantry. Don't forget receptacles for appliances and phone chargers or the like. If space is tight, a pocket door might be the solution and will allow for a bit more ventilation, as will a louvered door.

• walk-in pantries

For walk-in pantries and pantries built into closet-size spaces, shelves that are waist high and taller should be 6 in. to 9 in. deep. For lower shelves, set around 2 ft. above the floor, a 16-in.-deep shelf works. It is also useful to put a 12-in.-deep shelf up high, where seldom-used items can be stored. Recycling bins, bulky items, and the vacuum cleaner can sit on the floor. To make sure your pantry accommodates the way you live, wait until the drywall is up in the space, then pencil in where shelves should go based on your actual reach and the items that really will be stored.

FACING PAGE LEFT This beadboard-paneled walk-in pantry offers amenities similar to those of a butler's pantry. There's a countertop for working, a microwave, and dish storage. Hidden from view are open shelves for traditional pantry items. An operable window keeps the space ventilated.

FACING PAGE RIGHT A multi-purpose walk-in pantry has space for surplus appliances like a toaster, spices and jars of dry ingredients, and oversize dishes and tools, as well as a host of storage baskets. Lights installed above the countertop and natural light from a glass-block window add warmth to the space.

RIGHT High on the priority list for this renovated San Francisco Bay Area kitchen was a pantry with instant accessibility. The doorless room includes fixed shelves for spices and condiments and a bookcase with open shelves and a base cabinet.

• butler's pantries

There are pantries and then there are butler's pantries. A butler's pantry is really a passageway between cooking and dining space, with gussied-up cabinets meant for storing and displaying dishes and glassware. Shelving, often open, is what unites the two kinds of pantries in purpose, but the butler's pantry is much more formal, usually with wood shelving, not utilitarian wire.

The butler's pantry needs to have a countertop for serving plates or that acts as a buffet. It may also be home to a small sink and a second dishwasher. As a rule, appliances aren't meant to camp out on the countertop in a butler's pantry, as they may in the kitchen proper. But if space is tight in the kitchen, a butler's pantry can become a second workspace such as a baking center, with a stand mixer at the ready.

ABOVE Color, lighting, a granite countertop, and a petite sink work together to make this butler's pantry a functional and stylish space. Fixed shelves positioned close together make it easy to load and unload dishes.

RIGHT In this coffee-station alcove just off a small family kitchen, open shelves made of solid wood are painted to match the engineered stone countertop. The aqua glass tile on the wall adds a cool, dramatic bank of color.

This traditional butler's pantry, just a few steps from the kitchen, includes handsome cabinetry for dishes and silverware and a rich wood countertop. Open shelves offer storage and display space for books, CDs, and office supplies.

RIGHT This well-organized pullout pantry makes good use of every inch of space. A horizontal pull that spans the width of the door allows the pantry to be pulled out without racking.

FAR RIGHT It's not in a room of its own, but this bank of cabinets adjacent to the dining area is a perfect substitute for a formal butler's pantry. Storage for glassware, a wood countertop, and a wine cooler are accompanied by a mirrored backsplash.

countertops, backsplashes & sinks

● ● ●

COUNTERTOPS, BACKSPLASHES, AND SINKS SEE THE MOST ACTION IN A KITCHEN, YET WE EXPECT THEM TO LOOK GREAT, TOO. Fortunately, there's no need to compromise appearance or performance. With today's counter-tops, sinks, and faucets, style and functionality go hand in hand. The backsplash isn't exposed to constant wear and tear, making it the perfect place to incorporate materials that are not practical to use on a flat surface. But that doesn't mean it won't be durable.

Nowadays, kitchens are where a variety of tasks take place, so it makes sense to equip countertops, backsplashes, and sinks with different materials and configurations. Think about choosing a marble top for a baking center and stainless steel for around the cooktop. A small sink for washing veggies and a larger sink for dishes wouldn't be a bad idea. Also keep in mind that each appliance needs a nearby countertop—15 in. if possible— as landing space. Each cook should be able to claim a 36-in.-wide countertop. As for height, a 36-in. countertop is standard, but you may want to consider a few countertops that sit higher or lower.

A sink is the hardest-working kitchen tool, so make sure it is comfortable for you. Consider size and configuration, then materials, accessories, and, finally, the faucet and other back-of-sink fixtures.

White materials incorporated throughout this kitchen make it a serene, airy space. Rectangular tile serves as a backsplash, and marble— square-profiled with eased edges on the perimeter countertops and ogee-profiled on the island—gives rich texture to the single color scheme. The primary sink is paired with an equally generous bridge faucet in polished nickel.

backsplashes and countertops

●●● COUNTERTOPS AND BACKSPLASHES ARE OFTEN MADE OF THE SAME MATERIAL; WHAT SETS THEM APART IS FUNCTION.

The countertop takes a beating with all the food prep that takes place on its surface. The backsplash has the less onerous job of protecting the walls from wayward spatters. The ideal countertop is smooth, flat, nonporous, and non-staining; the ideal backsplash resists stains and moisture, too, but needn't be smooth or flat (although a smooth surface is easier to clean).

A backsplash deserves to be a little, well, splashy. It is a great place for a design focus, such as a painting, bright color, patterned tile, or contrasting texture. A backsplash can be relatively small: a 4-in.-tall row of tile, a mini-shelf for holding spices, or a turned-up countertop lip. But for the most coverage, look for a backsplash that fills the entire area between countertop and cabinet bottom.

Countertop materials can be highly polished, matte, or even textured. Keep in mind that a highly reflective surface requires diligent upkeep and cleaning, and that scratches show clearly, whether on stone or stainless steel. If a shiny, unscathed countertop surface is important, make it mandatory that cooks use cutting boards. You'll also want to pay close attention to lighting, especially under wall cabinets, if you choose a highly reflective surface, as reflections may shine into the eyes of seated diners.

With today's ever-burgeoning marketplace of countertop and backsplash materials, looking at all your options can take forever. But take your time, because the countertops and backsplashes that finally make it into your kitchen should last for years. To make an informed decision, borrow, or even purchase, the largest samples you can find and live with them for a while. Take into consideration durability, ease of maintenance, looks, temperature (you'll want a cool surface for making pastry dough), and cost. And consider sustainability. Ask where the materials come from, how they are made, and, most importantly, if they will stand the test of time.

The focal point in this kitchen is the cherry baking table topped with a Carrara marble slab, perfect for rolling dough or making bread. Honed Italian limestone countertops with eased-edge square profiles complement the equally subtle high backsplash of square, pale green mosaic tile.

This gunmetal granite peninsula is multilayered for function and aesthetics, with the sink and surrounding workspace set lower than the dining and food-prep countertop. A skylight reflects light onto the brilliant turquoise mosaic tile of the sink alcove.

ABOVE In this Manhattan apartment, the texture of the exposed brick wall contrasts with the smooth, black granite countertop and stainless-steel appliances, but harmonizes with the warm cherry-colored cabinetry.

RIGHT A one-piece glass backsplash in milky white coupled with a white solid-surface countertop is both easy to clean and water resistant. Pairing bright white surfaces, including the tile floor, with solid, dark brown cabinets creates a crisp, tailored look.

Soft countertop materials like this solid-surface countertop are durable, but will get knicks and scratches if cut directly upon. This custom-fitted cutting board is a nice contrast to the dark countertops and muted cabinetry, and it provides a suitable surface for chopping and slicing.

Sink and countertop materials follow function in this spacious California kitchen. A 4-in. edge-grain countertop provides ample space for food preparation, then transforms into an informal dining table. Around the copper sink and atop the base cabinets across the aisle, an equally thick stone countertop provides a hardier surface for knife tasks and hot dishes.

A thick limestone countertop and foot-high backsplash work well with matte ceramic tile, and make for a heatproof cooking space. Limestone acquires a soft patina with use, enhancing the well-worn feel of this inviting kitchen.

ABOVE The neutral shades of the irregularly sized mosaic tiles in this backsplash match the colors of the cabinetry, countertop, and stained wood floor.

LEFT Mosaic stone tiles grouted with a neutral tan color give the opportunity to incorporate numerous colors while creating a surface that won't show stains—ideal for a backsplash behind a cooktop.

• tile

Tile has been in the kitchen forever, mostly because it is durable and keeps its good looks. These days it is usually showcased on backsplashes. But as a countertop material, tile has the advantage of economy and unlimited flexibility, as it can be found in just about any color, size, surface texture, and pattern. It is resistant to heat and more affordable than solid surfacing, stainless steel, slab or engineered stone. Keep in mind, however, that tile is a hard surface; things dropped on it tend to shatter and the tile itself can chip. Keep cutting boards at hand to prevent damage.

Glazed, porcelain, and glass tile are all nonporous (though stone tile requires a sealer), but the grout between individual tiles is not. In countertops and backsplashes, look into stain-resistant additives and color for the grout, and make joints as narrow as possible and be sure they are well sealed.

Three materials harmonize to make this handsome ensemble. The glass mosaic tile of the cooktop backsplash matches the colors in the granite countertop. Sealed limestone tile in a pale neutral covers the adjoining backsplash space.

RIGHT Thin, rectangular white tile makes an elegant backsplash for this cooktop. Irregular edges add a subtle sense of texture to the broad expanse. Behind a cooktop, use white grout with non-staining additives or seal the grout to prevent staining.

LEFT White subway tile and a curved-profile tile border provide flash. The plastic-laminate countertop offers the look of stone for a fraction of the cost.

Materials find common ground in color, with the tile backsplash a toasty gold, marble countertops an orangey yellow, and cabinets painted creamy white. Bronze knobs on the cabinets and drawers provide contrast.

Polished black granite reflects everything in this light-filled kitchen. The breadth of the countertop and location of a cooktop in the center suggest the granite was installed in three pieces of the same size.

STONE COUNTERTOPS

Stone has come into vogue with a vengeance. Granite, in particular, has supplanted plastic laminate as the countertop of choice in new and renovated kitchens. It is extremely hard and durable, is cold to the touch, and can withstand heat. Quarried all over the world, from Argentina to Italy, granite is available in almost any color and pattern.

Stone is prepared in two thicknesses: 2cm and 3cm. The depth of a stone countertop's edges, however, can be increased to 4cm so that the whole piece looks like a thicker slab. Edges range from a basic square to bullnosed to highly profiled edges that have a higher price tag. A stone's surface may be highly polished, honed (a less reflective, satiny finish that doesn't show smudges), or rough, which is fine for a backsplash but not for a countertop.

Remember that softness does not always relate directly to porosity. For example, soapstone is soft but less porous than most types of granite. It does not require sealing, but it does need to be oiled to keep from looking dull.

Many stones stain unless sealed on a regular basis. Sealer type and maintenance schedule depends on the stone. Stone prices vary widely. Square-footage estimates can be a start, but other factors can have a big effect on the final cost. The breadth and rarity, for instance, of a stone will determine the cost, as well as the amount of labor needed to make cutouts and seams. Seaming often reduces prices because the size of each stone is smaller, but too many seams can give a countertop an awkward appearance. It's a good idea to visit stone yards to see stones in person and choose the exact stones for your kitchen. Think about where the stones' seams must go. Fancy edge profiles such as ogee will cost more than a simple, eased-edge square profile.

BELOW The polished granite countertop on the kitchen island of this modern kitchen has a square profile with eased edges for comfort.

FAR LEFT Earth tones infuse this traditional kitchen with warmth, with light brown marble on the countertop and glazed tile in tan, red, and green on the low backsplash.

LEFT A marble-topped baking station becomes especially handy with an electronic scale built into the corner, at the ready for weighing ingredients.

• marble, limestone, soapstone, and slate

Marble and limestone are mainstay materials for backsplashes, and they make equally fine countertops. Both are softer and more porous than granite. They must be sealed upon installation and at regular intervals after that to retain their looks. Marble is soft and cool to the touch and a favorite of pastry-makers. It will, however, lose its luster and smoothness if exposed to acid, so be sure to wipe up after slicing tomatoes. Less commonly used is limestone, which is a muted cream color with bits of fossil and shell often visible on its surface.

Soapstone and slate are gaining popularity as countertop materials. They are softer than granite, so scratches can be sanded out. Both are also denser—less porous—than granite and, as a rule, do not require sealing (verify this before purchasing a specific stone). Soapstone comes in numerous shades of green and gray. It is light colored when first quarried and installed, darkens immediately and uniformly when rubbed with oil, and continues to darken over time. Slate colors are more varied: gray and gray-toned green, red, purple, and black.

FACING PAGE Soapstone surfaces on these counters and backsplash show rich veining, brought out by periodic applications of mineral oil; the tone will deepen over time. Stainless-steel wall ovens and an apron sink with a heavy-duty faucet and pull-down sprayer maintain the gray color palette.

BELOW Soapstone surrounds a porcelain farmhouse sink to signify the limits of the washup area in a beautifully crafted wood island with face-grain wood countertop.

Soapstone is a soft stone and relatively easy for a craftsperson to cut and shape, but it's also extremely dense, making it an ideal material for the countertop surrounding an undermount sink.

Honed slate makes an understated backsplash and elegant countertop, both of which contrast richly with the white woodwork. Ideal for around the sink, slate is dense and needs no sealing.

The countertops shown here are both engineered stone. The island prep surface features a light dappled pattern, and the side bar is outfitted with a darker surface.

• engineered stone

Engineered stone, or composite stone, looks similar to granite but is more uniform in pattern, without the random seams found in natural stone. Composite stone is man-made from 90 percent ground quartz or granite with a resin binder. Like granite, these materials are tough, durable, and heat resistant. They also have the added advantage of being nonporous. Many colors and patterns are on the market with polished, honed, or sandblasted finishes.

BELOW Engineered stone makes an impervious and heat-resistant countertop, even next to a range. Glass mosaic tile adds color and a focal point to the stone tile backsplash.

TOP LEFT The modern style of this North Carolina kitchen is established with a sleek countertop of engineered stone. The pale blue glass tile and custom-built frameless cabinets finish the look.

BOTTOM LEFT A closeup look at engineered stone—a long-lasting countertop material that doesn't require sealing—reveals a complexity of colors, the result of binding stone aggregate with pigmented resin.

• plastic laminate

Plastic laminate is second in popularity only to granite when it comes to new kitchen countertops. It's inexpensive, easy to install, easy to clean, and has good stain and water resistance, unless a seam is compromised. It does have a few vulnerabilities. Plastic laminate's thin top layer shows knife marks and scratches, and the surface does not withstand high heat. It is also not considered as stylish as it once was. But give plastic laminate a chance. There is a large range of colors and finishes available, including solid colors, ersatz stone, retro patterns, and polished and pebbled surfaces.

Plastic-laminate countertops with beveled edges are trimmed at the sides and back with blue-toned mosaic tile. The rest of the backsplash is painted drywall or paneling.

more about...
PLASTIC-LAMINATE COUNTERTOPS

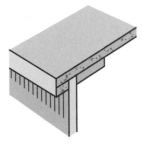

Square or self edge A square edge is the simplest and least expensive plastic-laminate edge, yet it offers a more contemporary look than a post-formed edge (similar to the post-formed cove).

Beveled edge A plastic-laminate molding with beveled edges is glued to the countertop to simulate a stone edge.

Post-formed cove Plastic laminate can be formed in a shop or factory to cover an integral 4-in. backsplash.

No cove Instead of having a post-formed cove, a plastic-laminate countertop can be completely flat with a backsplash of any material covering the back edge.

Applied wood or metal edge An applied edge of wood or metal gives plastic laminate a custom look. The edging can be straight, beveled, bullnosed, ogee—any profile that suits.

solid-surface countertops

Solid surfacing is a workable and homogenous material, so edges can take on just about any profile.

Integral backsplash A solid-surface countertop can be made with a 4-in. integral backsplash for added protection from spills.

 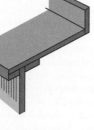 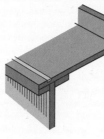  

Square edge The standard profile for a single-thickness, solid-surface countertop is the square edge. A single-thickness can also be shaped into a bullnosed, beveled, ogee, or other more complex profile.

Doubled edge A double layer of solid-surface material at the overhang gives heft to the countertop.

Inlay detail Stripes or complex details can be inlaid in solid surface in the shop or factory.

Doubled bullnose This bullnosed, double-layered edge adds to the stonelike appearance of the solid-surface pattern.

Complex profile The top layer has an ogee profile and the bottom has a Dupont profile, just one of several available profile combinations.

• solid surfacing

Solid surfacing, another synthetic countertop option, is made with polyester or acrylic resin mixed with a mineral filler. It can be shaped into pretty much any edge profile and any configuration, including countertops with integral sinks and backsplashes. It is completely nonporous, doesn't release odors, is easy to clean, and is reasonably resistant to heat (but not to super hot pots). Because solid surfacing is homogenous and fairly soft, it is easy to repair and gentle on dropped dishware. Solid-surface options—now in a wide variety of colors and finishes—run in the middle of the pack. It is less expensive than stainless steel, concrete, and most stone, but more expensive than laminate, tile, and most wood species.

This solid-surface countertop is easy to clean and maintain, and is suitable for food prep and informal dining. The island is finished with baseboard rather than toespace, so a deep overhang was added for comfort.

Multiple surfaces make this eclectic kitchen functional, too. Thick edge-grain mahogany countertops are used for dining and serving space. Granite surrounds sink and cooktop, while stainless-steel tiles make a glittery but durable backsplash.

• wood countertops

Food-preparation surfaces made of wood have been around for centuries—it's just that people called them tables. Yet wood countertops have fallen out of fashion of late because of their need for attention and upkeep. Thankfully, the recent trend of matching materials to functionality has revived the appeal of wood countertops. Wood makes a beautiful countertop that is hardworking as well, and many species of wood are less expensive than stone or solid-surface. Wood is easy to work and shape. It is also soft to the touch, gentle on dishes, can survive moderate heat, and is easily repaired with sanding and oiling. It develops a patina over time, or can look like new with regular maintenance.

Any species of wood can make a decorative countertop, but tough woods like maple are the best for butcher-block countertops. Both end-grain and edge-grain butcher blocks make good cutting surfaces, while face-grain wood works well as a serving or dining countertop. Work-surface wood countertops are typically left unsealed and maintained with periodic rubdowns with mineral, tung, linseed, or other nontoxic oils. Drying a wood countertop after it gets wet helps maintain its surface. Wood that won't be used as workspace can be sealed with polyurethane. It is also a good idea to finish the underside of the wood to prevent warping.

TOP The mahogany-topped dining areas in this kitchen are welcoming and create a close connection to the living room. A polished granite countertop provides a durable surface for food preparation.

BOTTOM The prime kitchen workspace of this renovated farmhouse is a 4-in.-thick face-grain wood countertop. It wears a patina on its surface created from preparing many family meals.

CARE

For wood countertops used in food preparation, rub with food-grade oil (mineral oil is typical) as often as needed, and don't use detergents. Make sure to wipe up any liquid on the surface of the wood immediately. Wood surfaces that won't be used for food can be finished with polyurethane.

GRAIN

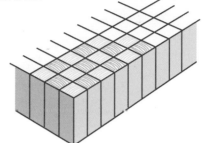

End-grain butcher block An end-grain butcher block makes a strong surface for chopping.

Edge-grain butcher block Edge-grain butcher block makes a surface that is less porous and not quite as tough as end-grain block. Hard maple is commonly used for its strength and dense grain.

Face-grain Face-grain boards are not as strong as end- or edge-grain boards, particularly for cutting, but they do make handsome surfaces for serving and dining.

EDGE PROFILES

Wood countertop edges can be given any profile, including square (also called flat), square with eased edges, radiused, bullnosed, and ogee.

•metal countertops

Stainless-steel countertops are found in almost every professional kitchen in the world. Stainless steel is resistant to heat and knife marks. It is durable, nonporous, and easy to keep clean. Because it's a malleable material, it can be formed with an integral sink or backsplash. If it has a brushed surface, fingerprints and scratches are disguised. With so many assets, it is no wonder that homeowners want the same ease and style of stainless steel in their own kitchens.

If you decide stainless-steel countertops are right for your kitchen, 16-gauge to 14-gauge steel (the lower the number, the thicker the steel) is best for a sturdy countertop. Remember that a stainless-steel countertop is formed around or supported by wood or medium-density fiberboard to add strength and mute sound. While stainless is unaffected by hot pans, be wary of putting very hot cast-iron pans on zinc or copper surfaces; discoloration may occur. Unless scrupulously polished, copper and zinc will acquire a patina, either over time or after exposure to heat or certain chemicals.

A custom-fabricated stainless-steel countertop with a 4-in. backsplash and integral sink makes a waterproof assembly. Stainless steel is also heatproof and easy to sanitize.

A stainless-steel countertop can be home to an integral custom-made sink, but a less pricey and almost-seamless alternative is attaching a manufactured stainless-steel sink to a stainless countertop.

gallery

metal countertops

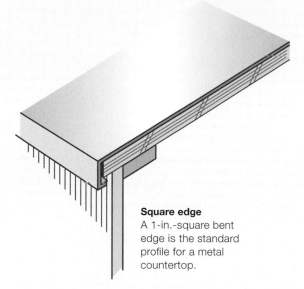

Square edge
A 1-in.-square bent edge is the standard profile for a metal countertop.

Integral backsplash The most waterproof of all countertop details is the integral backsplash, easy to form in metal. The backsplash can cover the whole wall area or come up 4 in.

Wood trim For a softer look, a metal countertop can be bent over the substrate and covered with wood trim. More maintenance is required to keep the joint clean.

Quilted backsplash A quilted metal backsplash—or metal tiles—offers the same water and heat resistance as a metal countertop, but adds a bit of visual variety.

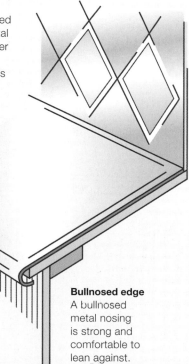

Bullnosed edge
A bullnosed metal nosing is strong and comfortable to lean against.

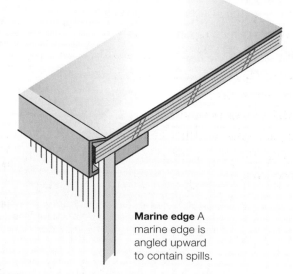

Marine edge A marine edge is angled upward to contain spills.

Recycled-glass countertops are similar in heft to engineered stone and solid surface. Cement-bound glass is tough but requires a sealer, while resin-bound counters don't need sealing but do require trivets for hot pots and cutting boards for food prep.

• concrete, paper, and glass

Countertop materials made of concrete, paper, or glass are conglomerates of small and ground-up materials, some man-made and some not. Concrete is a design favorite and, if carefully planned and cast, makes a beautiful countertop. It takes any color, texture, and shape, and any number of objects can be cast into it—from glass pieces to whole shells. But concrete stains easily, so it must be sealed carefully and periodically with either a topical or a penetrating sealer. It's critical to find a reputable craftsperson to make a concrete countertop, so ask for references and look at sample work.

Has-been concrete can be ground up and bound with resins or cement and made into a new countertop. This allows the concrete to take on a second life as a countertop material that is less prone to staining than the original.

Concrete isn't the only material that can have a second life in another form. Materials as diverse as recycled glass, shredded aluminum, paper, and plant pulp can be bound with resin or cement to form tough, durable, and good-looking countertops. Prices vary but tend to be slightly more affordable than stone and solid surfacing.

Paper-based countertops are durable, stain-resistant if finished and maintained properly, and come in many colors. Scratches are easily sanded out, but stay noticeable, and may require that the entire countertop be refinished at the same time.

Recycled glass, bound with epoxy resin or cement, makes a gorgeous countertop. Cement-bound surfaces are more durable but require a sealer. Resin-bound counters are not as durable but need no sealing (they do require waxing for shine).

TOP This sleek concrete countertop was cast in sections for ease of installation and to prevent cracking. It was sealed on site.

BOTTOM Green-tinted concrete countertops create a strong aesthetic in this house built with sustainable materials. Matching mosaic tiles add texture to the backsplash, and the raised countertop is recycled glass.

sinks

● ● ● A SINK IS FAR AND AWAY THE HARDEST-WORKING KITCHEN TOOL, SO IT'S IMPORTANT TO MAKE IT WORK FOR YOUR KITCHEN NEEDS. Consider size and configuration, then materials, accessories, and the faucet and other back-of-sink fixtures. One large sink can be made into a double sink by installing a dishpan or dish rack, leaving room for half-sheet baking pans, grill racks, and big stockpots. A two-bowl sink isn't as flexible.

Don't let convention determine sink location. In front of a window may be the perfect spot for a sink, but overlooking the rest of the kitchen or family room may work better for you. Wherever the sink goes, make sure there is at least 2 ft. of countertop space on both sides for dishes and food prep.

The custom-fabricated under-mount stainless steel sink in this kitchen features two bowls, so dishes can conveniently soak on one side while breakfast cereal bowls are washed in the other. The raised countertop is high enough to shield a sink full of dishes from view, but low enough to allow cooks and guests to chat with ease.

A broad porcelain-enamel undermount sink in white is a tailored choice to pair with the polished black granite of the surrounding countertops. The dark bronze faucet and water filter add a metallic luster to the space.

FACING PAGE This porcelain farmhouse sink was rescued from a salvage yard and reglazed for use in a 19th-century cottage. A brushed-nickel bridge faucet and pale green mosaic tile backsplash complete the traditional look.

• prep sinks

Do you need a prep sink? If it will be used mostly for filling pots or teakettles, a pot-filler may do the trick. A pot-filler is a long-armed, cold-water-only faucet that extends from a wall to fill a pot and can be pushed out of the way, against the backsplash, when not in use. If you want hot and cold water, and an extra basin to wash vegetables, a small prep sink may be the right choice.

Most cooks would agree that a prep sink should be close to the cooktop and next to the main prep surface, but the position also depends on how you cook and how many cooks you have in the kitchen. Make sure there is room for trash receptacles near food-prep stations. If sinks are far apart, you may want to consider the convenience of two trash centers rather than one central location.

Installed in a short but handy peninsula, this undermount stainless-steel prep sink is deep enough for serious washing. A metal rack helps prevent dishes from breaking.

FACING PAGE A prep sink is a splurge that pays the cook back in convenience. This round sink is just right for rinsing fresh produce that can go straight to a waiting pot or pan on the cooktop.

ABOVE A generous stainless-steel apron sink, undermounted to honed Italian limestone, accommodates pots or pans of any size. The tall brushed nickel faucet balances the sink's wide expanse.

all about...
SINK MATERIALS

Stainless steel is nonporous, easy to clean, tough, and immune to heat, and it won't rust—that's why it's the most popular sink material. A 7- or 8-in.-deep rectangular single-bowl sink made of 18-gauge steel is an all-around good choice—economical, durable, and big enough for most any job. But you may prefer a 16-gauge sink (remember, the lower the gauge, the thicker the steel) in a multiple-bowl configuration.

There are many shapes and sizes of stainless-steel sinks—from apron-front to square-cornered to those with integral backsplashes—but if you can't find the perfect model, look for a local shop that can custom-fabricate a sink. Keep in mind that sinks with sharp inside corners may look stylish but are hard to clean. As a compromise, look for sinks with slightly curved corners.

Like an integral stainless-steel sink in a stainless-steel countertop, an integral solid-surface sink is a waterproof choice, and it's quieter than stainless. Ceramic, enameled cast-iron and enameled steel sinks are easy to clean and don't scratch easily, but may chip. Enameled cast-iron sinks are eye-catching, pleasingly plump, and appropriate for a country kitchen, but keep in mind that cast iron is merciless when it comes to dropped dishware.

TOP LEFT A custom-fabricated stainless-steel countertop with integral sinks and backsplashes could easily work in a restaurant, but the setup is also perfectly suited for this kitchen, which is styled for an early-20th-century English manor.

BOTTOM LEFT Merging farmhouse style with modern efficiency, this porcelain-enamel cast-iron apron sink sits in a custom-fabricated stainless-steel countertop. The drain is set to one side so that pans can soak at the other end.

The sink, countertop, and backsplash in this kitchen are Vermont slate—a dense, soft stone that requires no sealing. Carefully adhering and sealing individual slate pieces makes this an integral, watertight group.

Clean lines, no seams, and easy maintenance steered the design choice for this kitchen sink. The integral solid-surface sink and countertop are a good match for a serious cook.

A sink with dividers and two faucets allows two people to work together and share the view. Single levers are easy to manipulate and require fewer holes cut into the stone backsplash.

•sink configurations

Much about the sink that will work for you depends on your cleanup habits. If every pot and pan goes straight into the dishwasher, you may not need a dish drainer, which would fit in either a two-bowl sink or a wide rectangular sink. If you use a lot of extra-large cookware, you may prefer a sink wide enough to fit a large baking sheet or roasting pan. If so, when budgeting, make sure to note that a sink wider than 33 in. will require a wider-than-standard sink base cabinet. Sinks with extremely curved inside corners may look spacious but may not accommodate large pans, so take your biggest roasting pan with you to the showroom to make sure it won't be a too-tight squeeze. Sink details make a big difference in performance. Sink drains, for example, don't always have to be installed in the middle of a sink basin. A drain that is off to the side makes it easy to soak a pan while allowing room for sink grids or racks that won't cover the drain.

Apron-front sinks, also called farmhouse or farm-style sinks, make it easier to belly up to the sink because there's no intervening countertop—just the sink edge. Undermounting a sink gives it more depth.

Sink prices can vary from $50 to $5,000, depending on material, size, and installation requirements. Typically, stainless steel, enameled cast iron, and solid-surface sinks are mid-priced. Basic stainless-steel sinks are, of course, more affordable than custom-made models of the same material with matching backsplashes and aprons.

sink types

Drop-in or self-rimming sink Countertop materials that have a weak edge, such as plastic laminate or wood, require a self-rimming sink. Steel sinks can be clipped into place and trimmed with a separate stainless-steel rim or they can be self-rimming, a neater but more expensive option. Porcelain-enamel cast-iron sinks remain in place solely by their weight. The raised rim of a drop-in or self-rimming sink makes it tough to sweep crumbs and trimmings into the sink, and it requires a little more elbow grease to clean, as the perimeter seam is exposed. All drop-in and self-mounting sinks should be sealed under the lip with silicone caulk.

Undermount sink Undermount sinks make it easy to clean off the countertop, but require a bit of attention to keep the top edge of the sink clean. Materials that require sealing, such as granite and marble, must be sealed at the cut edge. Heavy sinks require additional support from below.

Integral sink Stainless steel or other metal can be shop-made or manufactured into many configurations to accommodate an integral sink, backsplash, and countertop. Solid-surface and composite stone countertops can be shop-fabricated with integral sinks. These sinks have no joints, so they can't leak and there are no joints to clean around.

Farmhouse or apron sink The farmhouse, or apron, sink makes a statement in the kitchen, as it protrudes from the countertop and cabinetry. Its material and finish become prominent design features. These sinks make it easy to wash produce or dishes because of their generous size and forward placement. But farmhouse sinks also tend to be costly, in terms of both fixtures and cabinetry.

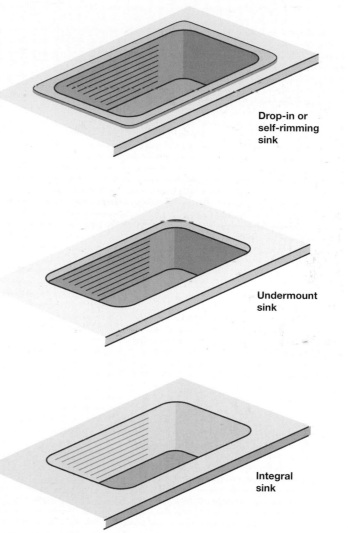

Drop-in or
self-rimming
sink

Undermount
sink

Integral
sink

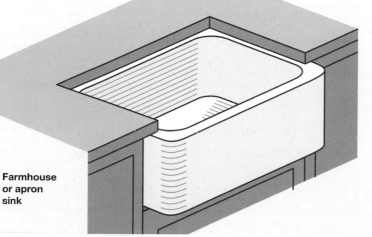

Farmhouse
or apron
sink

faucets

● ● ● FAUCETS CAN BE INCREDIBLY EXTRAVAGANT OR SIMPLE AND SERVICEABLE. There's no going wrong with a modest, low-rise faucet with a single-lever handle, and there are many finishes and styles that cost less than $200. Two-handled models are available for even less—or much more if you want a high-style bridge faucet, in which the cold and hot water supplies form a bridge between the handles under the faucet. A motion-sensor faucet or a faucet fitted with a foot-pedal control allows no-hands operation. In a kitchen with two cooks and only one sink, an extra-wide single sink or two-bowl sink may warrant two faucets.

Half of what makes a faucet great can't be seen, which means you want to know what to ask for. Faucets with ceramic discs won't wear out like ones with rubber washers. A solid brass or stainless-steel body will make the most durable faucet. Solid brass is always coated, and the toughest coatings have a PVD (physical vapor deposition) finish. Stainless-steel faucets, considerably more expensive than brass-bodied faucets, need no coating. They can have a high-polish finish or one brushed to a variety of textures.

Not just for beer taps, stainless steel and white porcelain levers complement this petite undermount prep sink and white marble countertop.

This no-fuss faucet blends a traditional two-handled bridge style with a quality sprayer, which slips out of its gooseneck channel for flexibility.

FACING PAGE
A curvaceous single-lever faucet with matching sprayer and soap dispenser make elegant fittings for twin undermount sinks. Shiny chrome and polished black granite light up the room.

ABOVE A low bridge faucet serves a island-based sink with grace and subtlety. Accessories such as this sink-spanning strainer add versatility to a big single-bowl sink.

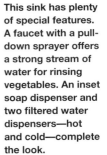

This sink has plenty of special features. A faucet with a pull-down sprayer offers a strong stream of water for rinsing vegetables. An inset soap dispenser and two filtered water dispensers—hot and cold—complete the look.

LEFT There's no clutter behind the sink of this wall-mounted faucet to block the view of the outdoors, reflected in the glass backsplash. The minimal single-lever handle is easy to operate and works well in this modern kitchen.

FACING PAGE This kitchen features a stainless-steel single-lever faucet for quick and easy operation at the sink. The integral solid-surface of the sink and surrounding countertop offer seamless cleanup.

• sprayers

Sprayers are a mighty handy faucet feature, and there are several flexible kinds. Faucets that morph into sprayers can have a visible flexible hose (professional-kitchen style) or a pullout hose from the base of the faucet. For cooktops that are not close to the sink sprayer, consider a pot-filler, a rigid faucet that swings out from the backsplash near or above the cooktop. The height of a pot-filler depends on the backsplash material, the height of your tallest pot, the height of the burner grates, and the location of the hood and any hood accessories. A pot-filler faucet requires a cold-water supply, which should be factored into the construction schedule as well as your budget.

ABOVE This pot-filler faucet fills the tallest pasta pot directly on the cooktop. The marble backsplash was designed and seamed to show off the veining in the center panel.

RIGHT A heavy-duty flexible hose makes rinsing vegetables and cleaning pots a breeze, but it does need to be paired with a deep sink to keep spray under control.

The tile panel of small mosaic glass made the installation of this pot filler fairly straightforward. Larger ceramic tile looks best when attachments such as a faucet or receptacle are installed at a joint or in the center of a tile.

A rectangular, single-bowl, stainless-steel sink is undermounted and flush with the surrounding counter of honed black granite. Minimal space and a modern aesthetic make the streamlined single-lever faucet with sprayer an ideal choice.

appliances

● ● ●

THERE WAS A TIME WHEN KITCHEN APPLIANCES MATCHED DOWN TO THE LAST DETAIL, BUT NOT ANYMORE. Increasingly specialized and unique, appliances come in all shapes and sizes and are easily mixed and matched. But appliances can also hide in plain sight, resembling cabinetry with the addition of panels or doors.

Appliances, with all their beauty, bells, and whistles, can make us sensible people lose our heads. What causes it may be as simple as the color of knobs or as complex as a multifunction oven. And who can blame us? After all, food and cooking (and cleaning up) are what kitchens are all about. So revel in it—make several trips to appliance showrooms, and spend some quality time poring over Web resources, including the ENERGY STAR site, which offers energy-saving tips and purchase suggestions for energy-efficient dishwashers, refrigerators, and freezers.

On top of it all, it's critical to coordinate appliances with countertop heights and cabinet dimensions, as well as with electrical and plumbing services. And remember that appliances aren't always immediately available and sometimes parts are back-ordered, so it's wise to include ample lead time in your schedule before installation and use. In other words, you may be eating take-out for a while, but it will be well worth it when your kitchen is ready for action.

This bank of appliances is built against an inner bearing wall and faces a wall of windows tucked above base cabinets. The central cutout offers landing space for dishes from the ovens or fridge and access to guests in the living room. A pullout cutting board offers additional prep space.

refrigerators and freezers

●●● EVERY KITCHEN HAS ONE, but nowadays—with the wide range of choices in size, configuration, and detailing—no two refrigerators are alike. There's the standard fridge-and-freezer combo, which can have the freezer on top, side, or bottom. With a bottom freezer, there can be a single door or French doors, a rightfully popular design that applies the narrow door swing of a side-by-side to a full-width refrigerator space. Bottom freezers can also be split into two compartments. All-freezer models paired with all-refrigerator types provide maximum cold storage space. Refrigerators and freezers installed beneath a counter provide close-at-hand storage space, whether it's for kids' snacks or tonight's dinner. With entertaining in mind, look into wine coolers and mini icemakers, both of which come in many widths and heights.

ABOVE The refrigerator as armoire is a design focus in this elegant kitchen with old-world style. Flat-top refrigerator doors with arched panels are combined with freezer drawers fitted with pulls identical to those used on all the cabinets.

RIGHT Behind these Shaker-style inset doors with chalkboard panels is a built-in refrigerator; below are two freezer drawers. The refrigerator hides in plain sight near the island and dining room.

ABOVE Refrigerator drawers provide supplementary storage to the primary refrigerator or freezer. These stacked drawers are built into the kitchen's island and are faced with matching white doors. Brushed nickel pulls resemble the refrigerator pulls.

LEFT A bank of cabinets with storage options: open shelves, floor-to-ceiling pantry, and two bays of cold storage—a refrigerator and wine cooler with additional freezer and refrigerator drawers underneath.

•fridge fit

How a refrigerator fits alongside cabinetry is a matter of aesthetics and budget. The standard fridge is 27 in. deep and standard cabinets are only 24 in. deep. This means that when a refrigerator is in position it juts out some 3 in. farther than cabinets. A pricey alternative that allows the refrigerator to blend seamlessly with cabinets is a cabinet-depth refrigerator, which is built at 24 in. deep. Another way to go is with a built-in fridge that is designed specifically for your kitchen and can be paneled to resemble cabinetry or finished with stainless steel or the more traditional black or white.

Cabinet-depth fridges make locating and retrieving food easier than standard-depth

refrigerators, but, on the other hand, you may not be able to fit a baking sheet or party tray into the former without moving stuff around.

It's easy to find refrigerators in some pretty snazzy enamel colors; you'll want to be confident of your choice, as you'll be living with it a long time. Even though it is very popular, stainless steel still adds to the price of a refrigerator. It also requires special polish and takes more time to clean than other finishes. Brushed stainless, which doesn't show fingerprints like polished stainless steel but still adds a professional panache to a kitchen, could be a better choice for your refrigerator.

A full-size built-in refrigerator and matching freezer is a prominent design element in this large kitchen. Positioned off to one side, it allows quick access away from any serious cooking that takes place.

ABOVE The big stainless-steel refrigerator amidst white cabinetry makes a bold statement in this renovated country house. Freezer drawers outfitted with one-piece drawer fronts blend with the surrounding pantry doors.

LEFT Freestanding appliances are sometimes more economical than built-in pieces, and they can be accommodated by a number of cabinetry designs and layouts. The cabinets surrounding this French-door refrigerator are built deeper so nothing juts out, and the microwave shelf holds a standard-size unit.

all about...
GREEN REFRIGERATORS

t o find the most energy-efficient refrigerators and freezers, first compare the energy statistics found on the EnergyGuide, a yellow tag attached to new fridges. (It also appears in product literature in print and online.) Here are a few additional rules of thumb. This one is sure to come as no surprise: Larger refrigerators use more energy than smaller models. Also keep in mind that fridges with top freezers are the most efficient models and that side-by-side refrigerators are the least efficient. In-door ice and water dispensers add 15 percent or more to a refrigerator's energy use (and are the prime reason for service calls). Keep in mind that the easier it is to retrieve food, the less time the door stays open, so consider models with pullout and elevator shelves, see-through drawers, and good lighting. New refrigerator models with more efficient compressors and better insulation are much more energy efficient than their forebears, so updating your old icebox can give your kitchen a style lift while helping to lower your energy bill.

Side-by-side refrigerators are the easiest models to fit with ice and water dispensers, though these add-ons consume plenty of energy. For easy access, this refrigerator is just around the corner from the dining room, as is the wine cooler and glass cabinet.

LEFT A beverage refrigerator like this one, with a reeded glass door for tempered visibility, reaches cooler temperatures than a wine cooler. An icemaker off to the side assures that drinks stay cold even longer.

RIGHT This newly installed built-in glass-door refrigerator is ready for stocking. Glass makes it easy to take quick inventory before heading to the store, but requires more attention to keeping contents looking presentable.

dishwashers

● ● ● WHEN CHOOSING A DISHWASHER, LOOK INTO CLEANING ABILITY, NOISE LEVEL, STORAGE CONFIGURATIONS, AND FINISHES. The standard dishwasher is 24 in. wide, but slimmer 18-in. models and wider models, up to 30 in., are out there. Double or single dishwasher drawers are generally for smaller loads, and are very energy efficient and space efficient (they can fit into just about any kitchen layout). Dishwasher drawers can serve as primary or secondary dishwashers, perhaps in a butler's pantry paired with a sink large enough for dishes and glassware, while a big sink and dishwasher in the kitchen handles pots and pans or party-size loads.

Evaluate a dishwasher's energy use by the amount of water it uses and how efficiently it heats water. Compare models based on water usage and the length of the washing cycle. Use the yellow EnergyGuide label as a guide. ENERGY STAR (a federal government program that tests and certifies products for energy efficiency) dishwashers use about a third less water than standard dishwashers. Keep an eye out for steam dishwashers as well. There are steam models on the market that appear to use much less water than most dishwashers (although they cost much more).

Two dishwashers, whether full- or drawer-size, offer increased storage space and flexibility— fill one with dirty dishes and take clean dishes from the other until it is empty. (The trick is to remember which is which.) There are plenty of different rack configurations for dishwashers, so when you are at the showroom think about the dishes you use most. Make sure the model you have in mind won't leave you hand-washing platters or pans.

FAR LEFT Concealed controls allow this dishwasher to blend seamlessly with the cabinetry. The single bin pull at the top looks like a variation on the knobs that adorn the other cabinets, but the location next to the sink is a giveaway.

LEFT Dishwasher drawers at an elevated position make loading and unloading dishes into nearby drawers an easy task.

Stainless-steel dishwasher drawers offer the opportunity to wash smaller loads and separate dishes according to wash-cycle levels. Gray-toned stone countertops and brushed nickel finishes on the cabinet hardware complement the stainless finish.

cooking appliances

●●● WITH SO MANY COOKING OPTIONS AVAILABLE, IT MAKES SENSE TO START WITH THE MOST BASIC CHOICE: a range or a cooktop with one or more wall ovens. Traditionally, a range is the more economical choice, but there are affordable cooktops and wall ovens out there. Separate elements spread out the heat source and require additional installation but allow for more flexibility when cooking. Of all cooking elements, cooktops see the most action, so it makes sense to choose a cooktop not just for looks but also for performance and ease of cleaning.

Don't forget to consider the little, but oh-so-important, details of a cooking appliance. You may prefer the tactile comfort of knobs to the precision of a digital touch pad. Easier-to-clean black, white, or colored enamel finish may be your preference over stainless steel. Cooking appliances are undergoing a dramatic transformation in appearance and technology, so you'll have plenty of options to sift through. Many devices cook cleaner and faster and combine fuel sources, such as a convection feature within a conventional radiant oven or a cooktop custom designed with modules that grill or steam.

Whatever the cooking appliances, it's imperative that there is adequate ventilation in the kitchen. Next, decide where a microwave oven will go, and whether or not a warming drawer, coffee center, or specialty cooking appliance makes sense in the scheme of things. As your plans finalize and appliances arrive, remember that safety should always be a priority, so buy one or more fire extinguishers and keep them handy.

A small speed oven does all the baking in this tiny house built by a retired couple with sustainable living in mind. Speed ovens offer three cooking modes: convection, microwave, and a fast-cooking combination of the two.

Venting a cooktop in an island requires extra power, but this sizeable column, which conceals structural supports and mechanical wiring, does the job of pulling steam and grease into the vent hood.

A vintage Wedgwood range inspired the traditional style of this kitchen, from the oak-door refrigerator and freezer components to the face-frame cabinets with latches, bin pulls, and baseboards. An out-of-the-way white microwave doesn't disturb the look.

A wall of stainless-steel appliances includes a refrigerator, espresso machine, convection oven, and warming drawer. A stainless-steel countertop offers a landing space for hot dishes.

• cooktop ventilation

Good cooktop ventilation is all about speed of airflow and configuration. A vent draws cooking smells, smoke, moisture, and airborne grease away from the cooktop. Grease is captured, and moisture and smoke are blown outside (the preferred method) or the air is filtered and recirculated into the kitchen. If a cooktop is situated on an exterior wall, venting to the outside is considerably easier. Built-in downdraft cooktop vents, which have a fan mounted under the cooktop, can pop up or be surface mounted. Pop-ups provide the more effective venting. Downdraft vents are less visible and less expensive than updraft vent hoods, but are much less effective.

In terms of speed of air flow, a vent fan should move at a minimum of 150 cfm (cubic ft. per min.). To vent a 36-in. cooktop, steer toward a 500 cfm to 600 cfm vent fan, which should handle the hot air, grease, steam, and odors produced while making a family-size meal. Keep in mind, however, that a strong fan needs a consistent supply of fresh air to replace the air that is pulled into the fan. You could open a window, but an air exchange unit built into the HVAC system, which mixes outside air with inside air, does this job better.

Speed of airflow isn't the only variable that determines how well a hood ventilates. A hood's size, placement, and configuration influence effectiveness, too. A hood should ideally be about 3 in. bigger than the cooktop, possibly more on an island cooktop, to inhale air most effectively. The higher the hood is above the cooktop, the wider it should be. Be aware that venting a cooktop in an island or on a peninsula is less efficient than venting a cooktop placed against a wall, as the wall helps contain and direct heat, moisture, and grease to the hood.

A large opening and strong fan allow this vent hood to be positioned farther above the cooktop than the recommended 36 in., thus maximizing the view. The convection oven and refrigerator are just a few quick steps from the island.

Cooking appliances are grouped on an outer wall in this North Carolina kitchen, making ventilation to the outdoors a direct affair. A stainless-steel backsplash and granite countertop offer tough, heat-resistant surfaces.

A bold design statement, this custom-designed hood is a sculptural element that is a necessity for serious cooking. Wider than the cooktop and 36 in. above the surface, the hood is sized appropriately for island cooking.

173

Operable by a remote control panel, this cooktop's downdraft vent elevates to vent odors and smoke. Its multilayer, removable mesh filter is dishwasher safe.

A ceramic tile shelf mortared into the backsplash and supported by hefty tile brackets puts pots and pans directly within reach of the professional-style range. The hood is sized for maximum efficiency and offers plenty of halogen task lighting.

The smooth electric cooktop with a ceramic-glass top is a subtle feature in this modern house but is built for serious cooking. Five elements combine to make seven cooking zones, all controlled from an electronic touch panel.

• ranges

The appeal of a range is that all the hot activities of a kitchen are concentrated in one place, and a standard range is usually less expensive than a separate cooktop and wall oven. But there are exceptions: Heavy-duty cast-iron models from Europe are quite expensive, but certainly stylish and hardworking. The standard, freestanding 30-in., 4-burner range usually has a single oven, warming drawer, and often a raised back guard. Some new ranges offer stacked ovens: a thin oven just below the stovetop that is great for making pizza, gratins, and cookies; and a standard oven underneath that large enough to roast a turnkey. Super-wide, pro-style ranges may have two ovens side by side.

Think twice before bringing a commercial range into your home. These appliances are not insulated and, because of the extreme heat they generate, are burning hot to the touch and can scorch adjacent cabinets. Instead, you may want to look into professional-style ranges, which are insulated and have pilotless ignitions. They also come with features not found in commercial ranges, such as oven windows, lights, and broilers. Look for the same design features that you'd want in a cooktop or wall oven, such as sealed burners and continuous grates or split oven racks and a covered electrical element.

This British-made range, cast-iron with small compartments for multidish cooking, is a dynamic, efficient appliance with traditional charm. This is an always-on model; for warm climates, dual-fuel ranges with electric ovens may be a cooler choice.

A professional-style range takes on a central role in this symmetrical design, with flanking windows, base cabinetry, and wall cabinets over the stainless-steel hood.

A 2-gallon-capacity steam cooker supplements this gas cooktop with the ability to steam vegetables and custards, proof breads, or act as a slow cooker.

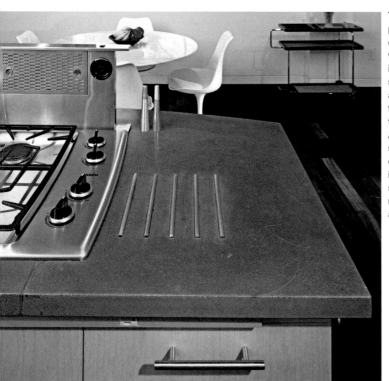

This 1½-in. precast slate-toned concrete countertop was molded with an integral stainless-steel trivet to make a safe landing spot for pots coming off the island cooktop. A receptacle strip below the countertop makes it easy to work with small appliances near the cooking action.

• cooktops

Cooktops can be fueled by gas (natural or propane) or powered by electricity (inexpensive electric coil, stylish electric smoothtop, and induction). Induction-powered cooktops are new to the market, but they have been well received. While electric, they are as responsive to temperature change as gas. They are also easy to clean and efficient, and expensive. Gas and electric cooktops have their admirers as well. Gas is instantly responsive and can be operated in a power outage. Continuous metal grates make it easy to drag pots from burner to burner, and closed burners make cleanup easier.

Electric coil and standard smoothtop cooktops are quick to heat but can be slow to respond to temperature adjustments. Smoothtops are easier to clean than coils; dark and speckled surfaces hide scratches and dirt better than white; a ceramic glass smoothtop requires more care when using heavy or rough-bottomed pots.

Look for a cooktop that has at least two high-powered burners and one that can keep liquids at a steady simmer. Take care where the cooktop is situated, as it will need a heat- and moisture-resistant backsplash. If you go for a professional-style gas cooktop with stainless steel aprons, remember that you'll need to coordinate the countertop height, cooktop height, and cabinet size to make sure that the cooktop ends up at the level you want it. Gas cooktops offer a variety of accessories, such as a grill, griddle, deep fryer, steamer, or wok.

Induction cooktops, operated by a high-powered electromagnetic field, are the latest in energy-efficient cooking. This model has four elements of varying sizes that can do anything from melting chocolate to sautéing vegetables.

INDUCTION COOKTOPS

Powered by electromagnetic energy, which causes ferrous (iron-based) cookware to heat, induction cooktops are almost twice as energy efficient as gas or traditional electric cooktops. This means that a large pot of water that comes to a boil in 10 to 14 minutes on a gas or standard electric cooktop will need only half that time on an induction cooktop. Induction burners are topped by a ceramic-glass surface similar to that of a smoothtop electric cooktop. Induction cooktops respond quickly and heat rapidly. They also provide consistent heat but don't heat the air,

and they offer easy cleanup, since spilled food won't burn and stick to the cooktop, which stays cool to the touch.

So what's the catch? Induction is pricey—as much as four times the cost of a standard electric cooktop (though it does cost less to run). Induction cooktops also require flat-bottomed ferrous cookware, so be sure to bring a magnet when you go shopping. If you are interested in what induction offers, look for single- and two-burner built-in cooktops, side-by-side induction-electric or induction-gas cooktops, or even a plug-in portable countertop unit.

A two-burner induction cooktop built into the island in this kitchen supplements a gas cooktop. Because it's cool to the touch even when the power is on, an induction cooktop makes a safer choice for use in an island.

• ovens

You can afford to be choosy when it comes to selecting an oven because there are a lot of options out there. Let's start with the standard oven—usually a radiant or thermal oven. This means food is cooked using radiant energy from a heat source, either an electric element on the bottom and top (for broiling) of the oven or a gas-fired flame under the oven floor. Another type of oven is the convection oven, which is an electric radiant oven outfitted with a fan to circulate heated air. True convection ovens feature a third heating element that heats air prior to circulating it. They are also more efficient and more expensive.

New oven technologies have diversified what is available on the market. Most intriguing to avid cooks in a hurry are speed ovens and steam ovens (steam ovens are often categorized as a type of speed oven). Speed ovens use several technologies—microwave, steam, convection, and high-intensity radiant heat such as halogen bulbs. Of course, increased speed and great cooking results come with a high price tag, but prices may come down as such high-tech appliances become more common. Steam ovens incorporate steam from a reservoir or plumbed water line (the latter is more expensive). Hybrid steam-convection ovens cook with their two namesake technologies, but either function can be used alone. Manufacturers tout them as ideal for all foods.

Wall ovens can be installed in a number of places in the kitchen. They are available at all price points, and some new 30-in. and 36-in. ranges offer two ovens, usually stacked. Larger pro-style ranges and heavy-duty European models feature smaller ovens that come stacked and side by side. Don't dismiss a smaller oven out of hand. They are more energy efficient than larger models and retain moisture better, too.

A warming oven, also called a warming drawer, has been a standard feature in electric ovens for years, but today's stand-alone warming ovens come with a lot of bells and whistles. For starters, warming ovens perform the basic function of keeping foods at a regulated temperature, so they won't cool while the rest of a meal is prepared. But that's not all these gadgets do. Foods are kept moist or crisp depending on various setting. Cooks also use warming ovens to heat plates or coffee cups, defrost food, and dry bread crumbs. For ease of use, the best location for a warming oven is just below the countertop.

Steam ovens cook foods rapidly while retaining moisture and vitamins. This model includes a convection oven above the plate-and-cup warming drawer.

The professional-style range in this kitchen offers two ovens side by side, providing flexibility when cooking for dinner parties or holidays, as well as a place to warm dishes while the other oven does the cooking.

This built-in coffee center offers espresso with the touch of a button. Small niches showcase dishware and a generous countertop makes the space an elegant, impromptu dining area.

A warming drawer is handy to have in the kitchen year-round, not just at holidays. Food remains moist and stays at a safe-to-eat temperature until dinnertime, or plates can be warmed for a dinner party.

Clustering appliances in a single bank of built-in cabinets is a handsome, smart design solution. The center column is a recessed china cabinet with landing space for dishes fresh from the wall ovens, coffee center, or warming ovens. The broad island offers adjacent seating for meals and a workspace.

• microwave ovens

The presence of a microwave oven is a given in most kitchens. Sometimes it even serves as the primary oven, especially as new technologies wed the fast-cooking capabilities of the microwave with convection and steam-heat technologies, which boost the taste and appearance of food.

The big question is where to put the microwave, conventional or not. An over-the-range (OTR) microwave oven makes sense in a small kitchen with limited countertop space. In a larger kitchen, consider a spot that is easy to reach but out of the path of the primary cook. Built-in microwaves tend to be deeper than wall cabinets, so they are usually installed in base cabinets or tall banks of cabinets that also incorporate wall ovens. Microwave ovens also fit nicely into island cabinetry, away from where the main cooking is done but at hand so that diners can help with heating tasks.

FACING PAGE According to the cook in this family kitchen, installing the 30-in., manual-open microwave drawer was the best design decision she made for the room. It frees much-needed countertop space and small kids can use it easily.

BELOW A confluence of appliances puts a speed oven, wall oven, refrigerator, and freezer within arm's reach of the island cooktop. Stainless-steel and dark metal-faced frameless cabinets make a dramatic combo.

The small appliances and microwave are corralled together in a neat corner of this kitchen, designed for serious cooking and frequent entertaining. Adjoining countertop space provides room to whip up a midnight snack.

Where space is at a premium, a microwave oven below a built-in cooktop vent makes sense. Honed black granite makes a tough backsplash and counter.

floors, walls & ceilings

● ● ●

THREE BIG SURFACES—FLOORS, WALLS, AND CEILINGS—MAY SEEM TO PLAY SUPPORTING ROLES IN THE KITCHEN, but they take center stage when it comes to impacting looks and budget. You can accentuate these surfaces with color and texture or let them recede into the background with neutral tones and materials. The ideal kitchen floor is both attractive and serviceable, but the specifics depend on your preferences and lifestyle. You may decide to use different materials for different workspaces, such as tile in the cooking area and wood in the breakfast nook, but be sure materials are installed flush to avoid dirt-catching seams and tripping hazards. Keep in mind that floor installation is easiest when done at the beginning of the construction process because the room is empty, but it's vital to protect the new floor as the rest of construction proceeds.

Walls are chameleons—you can paint them any color, or finish them with paneling or tiles. Keep easy maintenance and aesthetics in mind as well as strength—you'll want sufficient blocking installed to support shelving and cabinetry. As you decide

Stainless-steel cabinets and modern light fixtures add contemporary flair in this California kitchen, but the overall European-farmhouse effect takes its cue from the wall, ceiling, and floor finishes: Walls are covered in limestone veneer, structural beams are rustic, and the floor is an elegant pattern of limestone pavers.

what to do with your wall surfaces, look up, too. High ceilings can be a blessing in the kitchen, but you may want to visually lower them with trim—perhaps picture molding at door height with a darker color painted below and a warm white above—or the opposite, depending on ceiling height, climate, and your aesthetic preferences. Of course, the bonus to painting walls and ceilings is that it won't break the bank to repaint next year when you decide that a light-blue ceiling is just the thing to brighten your morning.

flooring

●●● A KITCHEN FLOOR MAY NOT BE THE FIRST THING TO CATCH YOUR EYE, BUT IT SURE HAS A BIG IMPACT ON A KITCHEN'S OVERALL LOOKS, and it can make a big difference to your comfort, both in standing on it and maintaining it. Softer floors like wood and resilient flooring (and even an area rug) are comfortable for feet and backs, and more forgiving of dropped dishes. If durability and longevity are prime considerations, stone or tile may be top choices. The most affordable flooring options are sheet vinyl, laminate, and do-it-yourself tile. Engineered wood is less expensive than solid wood. Stone and ceramic, because of labor and cost of materials, tend to be priced higher. At first glance a few dollars' difference per square foot of flooring may seem like no big deal, but for covering an entire kitchen, it definitely adds up.

If flooring is installed first, labor fees are usually less because there isn't as much detail work involved. Whatever the material, any new flooring should be well protected for the rest of construction. If cabinets go in first and flooring is last, which is usually the case with resilient flooring, there's less of a chance the flooring will be damaged. After the flooring is in, take the time to put felt pads on the feet of all movable kitchen furniture, so no scuffs mar the new surface.

Refinished heart-pine boards in varying widths make a warm backdrop for the traditional cabinetry in this kitchen, and at the same time complement the newly exposed structure of the home.

LEFT In a Manhattan kitchen, cool gray stone tiles mimic the dark-stained wood parquet tiles in the entryway, but create a lighter surface that matches the stainless-steel appliances.

BELOW Cork is an affordable, cushiony flooring option. The warm tones of the tiles in this mudroom and kitchen are finished with polyurethane to make a water-resistant surface.

• wood floors

Not too long ago, it was hard to find a wood floor in a new kitchen. The flooring you would find in the kitchen differentiated it from the rest of the house. But now kitchens are intimately connected to the rest of the home, and that's largely why wood floors have made a comeback. Using the same flooring in the kitchen and living spaces connects the two. It also doesn't hurt that wood floors add warmth to a room and are quite durable, able to be refinished again and again.

Solid wood flooring is usually oak-strip flooring (¾ in. thick and 2½ in. wide). Wider planks give a more traditional look, but are more expensive as well. More affordable but no less beautiful are kitchen floors made from hardwoods such as maple, cherry, and hickory, or from traditional softwoods like heart-pine and fir.

Engineered wood has the same appearance as solid wood, but is actually made of plywood with a top layer of appearance-grade wood. This makes it more dimensionally stable than solid wood. Because the top layer is very thin, engineered wood can't be refinished nearly as many times as solid wood.

Another decision to make is whether to buy prefinished wood (solid or engineered) or finish the wood flooring after it's installed. You can walk on prefinished wood as soon as it's installed, and its finish is super-tough. But because it has joints, it is vulnerable to water damage. On the other hand, unfinished wood flooring must first be acclimated to house temperatures and humidity (this varies depending on flooring characteristics, but count on several weeks). Finishing takes a few days or more and may not result in a tough factory finish like that of prefinished wood. It does, however, provide better overall protection, as joints are sealed too.

The longevity of a wood floor is directly linked to upkeep. Frequent vacuuming and damp mopping, quick attention to spills, curbing dog and shoe traffic, and, ultimately, refinishing—all of these help keep any kind of wood floor looking good. Area rugs help, too. As with any surface, glossy finishes as well as very light and very dark tones show scratches and stains more than medium tones and satin finishes.

Stripes provide the unifying theme to a variety of finishes in this snug Bay Area kitchen. Corrugated galvanized tin siding makes a nice contrast to the diagonal pine-strip flooring and ceiling and exposed ceiling joists.

TOP Salvaged pine boards with a knotty, unique character give a patina to this traditionally styled kitchen.

BOTTOM Dark stained wood flooring makes a stylish setting for the custom-made white cabinets with furniture feet in this traditional kitchen.

all about...
BAMBOO FLOORING

t he appeal of bamboo is largely its cachet as a sustainable material coupled with its unique texture and appearance. Technically a grass, bamboo has much in common with wood—especially "timber bamboo," which is grown on sustainable plantations, mostly in China. It's the fastest-growing plant on earth so it might seem sustainable, but transportation costs reduce its "green" rating.

Hardness and durability vary among different species of bamboo, and not all types work well in the kitchen. It is not as hard as stone, but not as soft as resilient flooring. As a flooring material, bamboo is akin to wood in its ambience and comfort underfoot. Flag-grain bamboo is less durable than vertical-grain.

When purchasing bamboo flooring, look for strand bamboo. It has fine parallel lines similar to quartersawn oak. Bamboo can be floating, nailed, or glued down. Like standard wood flooring, it comes prefinished or can be finished in place.

Bamboo is comparable in price range to wood and, like wood, its prices vary according to the form of the material and construction method.

This bamboo flooring has a straight, fine grain resulting from the process of splitting and laminating fibers under pressure. Factory-coated with aluminum oxide for toughness, the boards are finished with polyurethane for moisture resistance after installation.

• tile and stone

Ceramic and stone tile have made classy, durable, and sanitary kitchen floors for centuries. Ceramic tiles usually start out white, but are then coated with a layer of colored glaze. In contrast, porcelain, quarry, brick, and, of course, stone tiles are colored throughout, not just on the surface, so chips are less apparent.

Any stone can be made into tile. Marble, limestone, granite, and slate are the most common. Stone (except slate) tile and unglazed tile require regular sealing. An appealing alternative to stone is glazed ceramic tile made to look like stone. These tiles are waterproof and resistant to staining. Maintaining ceramic tile floors is often a matter of keeping the joints between tiles sealed against moisture and stains. The narrower the joint and the bigger the tile, the less sealant is necessary. Tile and stone floors, though gorgeous and tough, can be uncomfortable to stand on for long periods of time, so the addition of area rugs provides a cushiony surface.

FACING PAGE Fine texture is a unifying design theme in this sophisticated city kitchen. Tiny rectangular tiles fill the backsplash. A minute texture on the granite tile walls and floor with a gentle wash of color complete the look.

RIGHT Set flush with surrounding cherry wood flooring, the stone tile in this kitchen is a sensible choice for a hardworking cooking zone. It works with the exposed brick backsplash and brings texture and contrast to the room.

The rosy tone of the mahogany siding, trimwork, and stools in this kitchen is picked up by the ceramic tile flooring. Both materials are ideal for a kitchen on Martha's Vineyard, where salt air and sand prevail.

The wide expanse of marble tile in this kithen provides a durable walking surface in a room made for serious cooking. The cool white color of the stone has an ageless appeal.

ABOVE Resilient sheet cork flooring blends beautifully with this kitchen's cherry cabinets, but also brings a bit of texture to the room. Green ceramic tile and mosic glass tile backsplashes continue the trend.

LEFT This cheery kitchen is filled with subtle contrast. The colorful ceramic tile accents on a field of smooth, white tile act as the backsplash. The patterned black-and-white linoleum tile floor contrasts boldly to the sedate cabinetry and ceiling treatment.

• resilient flooring

Resilient-flooring materials like vinyl, linoleum, rubber, or cork are big favorites in new kitchens because they are comfortable to stand on, easy to install, and relatively inexpensive compared to solid and engineered wood floors, stone tile, and many types of ceramic tile. Resilient flooring is available in tiles and sheets; some resilient materials are also available in floating-floor planks, which click together, just like laminate flooring.

Today's resilient flooring comes in countless styles and colors, and can provide green options as well. Cork is a sustainable bark.

Linoleum is made from natural ingredients, including limestone dust, linseed oil, cork, and wood.

Resilient-flooring finishes also leave a tough, long-lasting surface. Cork and linoleum are factory-sealed, but should also be sealed after installation to protect the joints from moisture. Vinyl flooring needs no finishing. Resilient-floor types will last longer if maintained by regular sweeping and damp mopping and if spills near seams are wiped up quickly.

• concrete floors

Concrete floors are a sophisticated element in any kitchen, but getting them right is not always easy. It is a long, detailed process to design, place, finish, and seal a concrete floor. If you go this route, it's critical to find a reputable craftsman or study proper procedures if you plan on doing it yourself. The appeal of concrete is that it can take on a multitude of colors, textures, and patterns—shiny+ and colorful or subtle with a soft sheen. Color can be added throughout the mix or on the surface of the floor, after it's in place, using powdered or liquid pigments.

Concrete is hard and durable, but will develop cracks. Joints help control where cracks occur; make these a part of the entire floor design rather than an afterthought. Concrete is also quite susceptible to stains, so it must be sealed regularly.

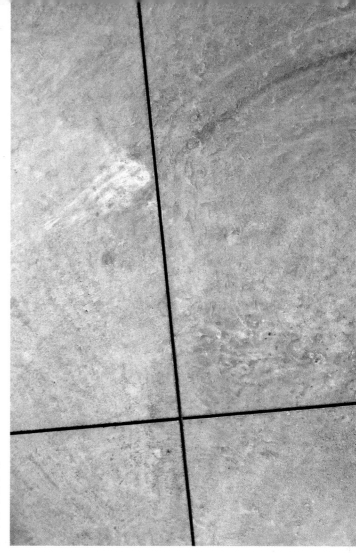

RIGHT Concrete is the chameleon of flooring materials. With a trowel, subtle colors were applied to this concrete floor before it cured, leaving a delicate sheen. Joints were cut after curing to control cracking.

LAMINATE FLOORING

a relative newcomer, laminate flooring has caught on quickly and is now the fastest-growing floor product available. The appeal of laminate is that it is affordable and can look like pretty much any material. A laminate-flooring plank is typically a layer of clear melamine laminated to a photographic image that is patterned, solid colored, or made to look like wood, tile, or stone. These top layers are laminated to a high-density fiberboard core and a moisture-resistant melamine backing.

Laminate-flooring planks or tiles are fitted together to float on a smooth, resilient underlayment. A thin material such as cork is the best—and most expensive—choice for underlayment. It cushions the planks and makes up for any unevenness in the subfloor. Planks fit together without glue, making them easy to replace and water-resistant, but not watertight, so it is important to wipe up spills quickly so water can't seep under the planks.

It is okay to window-shop online, but be sure to look and touch real laminate samples before buying, as larger samples will more accurately reveal what a finished floor will look like. For more realistic wood-like flooring, look for surface embossing that matches the texture you see in the photo layer. Another aesthetic might be to embrace laminate flooring as a synthetic material and select a solid color, or even several colors to make a striped floor. Choose thicker planks and thicker underlayment to make laminate flooring feel more solid underfoot.

walls and ceilings

●●● IN THE EARLY STAGES OF A KITCHEN-DESIGN SCHEME, DECISIONS ABOUT WALLS AND CEILINGS SHOULD BE CONSIDERED. Certainly paint, paneling, and even tile can be added later, but wall and ceiling configurations that require structural attention should not be left to chance. Also, a kitchen's lighting plans will have a direct effect on the ceiling style and design.

Walls don't need to have a uniform surface, but they can. Entire walls can be dressed in neutral colors or easy-to-clean wallpaper in bold floral or striped patterns, or wrapped in beadboard wainscoting for a traditional look. For paneling, trim, and walls, use satin or glossy paints, which are easier to clean than flat paints.

Look up at most kitchen ceilings and you'll find a smattering of recessed can lights in a flat, white ceiling. That is a fine finish for a kitchen with lots of design flash, but if you've got some vertical leeway, consider adding an ornate cove around the perimeter of the room or a curved ceiling across the span. Think about embellishing the top of a wall with a painted mural or wallpaper frieze. For the ceiling itself, paint could suffice, but you could also add beadboard paneling or embossed tin tiles. A dark ceiling adds coziness to a large kitchen, while a light-colored ceiling adds the illusion of height.

FAR LEFT
Wood tones with a hint of orange and bright turquoise mosaic tile make a compatible yet striking color pairing in this informal coastal kitchen.

LEFT The intricately arranged mosaic tile panel above the sink in this kitchen is a work of art. Grout sealer, which is brushed on and then wiped off the tile, helps prevent staining.

LEFT In this snug, well-used kitchen, chalkboard paint lets everyone make a mark and creates a quirky backdrop for an eclectic collection of dishes and cookware.

BELOW Corrugated metal adds a soft shine and an industrial flair to a small kitchen with wood finishes.

This gray tin ceiling would be oppressive in a kitchen with lower ceilings. But in this high-stature Victorian house, partnered with black cabinets and appliances and antique-yellow walls, it adds a glossy, old-world finish.

lighting & windows

● ● ●

LIGHTING—BOTH NATURAL AND ARTIFICIAL—IS THE SINGLE MOST
TRANSFORMING ELEMENT IN A KITCHEN. A well-lit kitchen brightens your day
as well as your tasks, and it makes all the difference in how welcoming the space is
to family and friends during meal preparation, socializing, dining, and even cleanup.
The key to a successful lighting scheme is providing light from several sources—
windows, high and low fixtures, and fixtures that are visible and hidden from view.
And every choice you make depends on the style, configuration, and tasks that take
place in your kitchen.

This chapter helps you understand types of lighting, and what fixtures and designs
allow you to achieve them. You'll come to see how dimming and varying sources
of light can change the mood of a kitchen, and what to do when a little more light
is called for. Most single-home kitchens include windows, but on an overcast day
and at night, lighting fixtures take over. Thankfully, lighting offers a big bang for the
buck. Unless you plan on springing for a showpiece chandelier, electrical fixtures
and wiring take up a small percentage of an overall design
and construction budget. And the thoughtful use of natural
lighting means savings on an electrical bill, as does the proper
placement and use of energy-efficient fixtures.

A serene kitchen with Craftsman details and color is spiced up with modern and traditional light fixtures. Traditional pendants work well with the modern undercabinet puck lights and recessed ceiling fixtures.

artificial lighting

●●● DESIGNERS DIVIDE LIGHTING INTO CATEGORIES, WITH AMBIENT, TASK, ACCENT, AND DECORATIVE LIGHTING FITTING THE BILL FOR MOST KITCHENS. Ambient light is general, allover lighting that warms a kitchen, disperses shadows, and makes it easy to move around. In the daytime, natural light provides most of the ambient light that a kitchen needs. At night, pendants or chandeliers, recessed and track lights, and fixtures hidden above cabinets will provide ambient light.

Task lighting shines where you work—at the countertops, range, sink, island, and desk. These lights should be as bright and natural in color as possible. Undercabinet fixtures, pendants, track lights, and recessed cans can give you the task lighting you need.

Accent lighting illuminates specific objects, such as decorative dishware, artistic objects, or architectural elements such as a column capital. Focused recessed fixtures, track lighting, in-cabinet fixtures, and sconces work as accent lights.

The best decorative fixtures look great on their own and serve another function, too, such as a wall sconce that provides ambient and accent lighting or a chandelier that offers ambient and task lighting. Wall sconces are prime examples of decorative light fixtures, which provide ambient, accent, and even task lighting, while adding style to the kitchen.

A cluster of three low-voltage pendant fixtures gives off a warm glow in this large kitchen with strong, traditional details.

Pendant halogen
fixtures provide
stylish task and
ambient lighting
above a primary
workspace in this
modern kitchen.

ABOVE Fluorescent fixtures with continuous plastic diffusers create accent strips at the edges of the kitchen, over the windows, and above the cabinets. At night, the strips provide ambient and task lighting.

LEFT A combination of skylights, surface-mounted adjustable cans, and under- and over-cabinet lights cast a favorable glow in this modern kitchen. The medium-dark Brazilian cherry floor balances the reflection cast off the many white surfaces.

all about...
LIGHTING CONTROLS

he best kitchen-lighting scheme is one that you can vary with ease. Automated control systems allow you to program lighting scenarios that are available at a touch of a button. Hugely convenient, these are also complex and expensive; wireless versions are even pricier. An economical alternative is to install rotary or slide dimmer controls (or pricier touch controls) for incandescent fixtures, and to provide switches and dimmers at the kitchen's main entry points. Keep an eye open for new fluorescent fixtures that are dimmable, too. Rather than deal with switches sprinkled throughout the entire room, cluster or stack them, whichever is more convenient and looks better to you.

A custom-fabricated light fixture covers most lighting types—ambient, task, and decorative—in a warm and stylish fashion.

•overhead lighting

Recessed downlights are perfect for just about any lighting needs, but it's a good idea to supplement them with other sources of lighting. Sort through the various bulbs, trim colors, reflector colors and sizes, and baffles available to see what style, size, and function suit your kitchen space. Space downlights approximately 4 ft. to 6 ft. apart so that light pools overlap on the countertop or floor.

Surface-mounted fixtures (also called flush- or ceiling-mounted) provide ambient and task lighting, and are themselves decorative. Examples include shallow fluorescent fixtures with white acrylic lenses, milk-glass schoolhouse fixtures, and oak-framed Arts and Crafts boxes.

Since the first white cans appeared decades ago, track lighting has evolved to include high- and low-voltage systems with pendants and adjustable spots. Track lights are individually adjustable and offer the full range of lighting—ambient, task, accent, and decorative. A variation on track lighting is the flexible rail fixture, which can be shaped any way to provide decorative, accent, and even task lighting. Low-voltage cable fixtures are taut cables that carry small decorative fittings, usually suspended over islands and tables.

ABOVE LEFT These low-voltage fixtures with red shades can be adjusted to any position along the rod. For their size, they pack a bright punch as task lights, and act as a decorative accent that coordinates with the colors in the mosaic tile backsplash.

Suspended low-voltage halogen fixtures have a strong profile and are easily adapted to different kitchen layouts. Fittings along the curved rod were adjusted so the lights would illuminate the workspace and cupboard.

RECEPTACLES

unless wireless technology takes over kitchen appliances, receptacles will find their way onto kitchen walls, so don't let them become an afterthought or eyesore. Plug molding, which runs along the underside of a wall cabinet or along the backsplash, has a subtle look and offers many places to plug in appliances. Note that wires hang down in plain view if appliances stay plugged in.

An alternative to incorporating wall receptacles into the backsplash design is accenting them with paint or camouflaging them with matching wallpaper. On a tile backsplash, take note of where receptacles will go; mosaic tile is more forgiving of receptacle placement than large tile.

In fixed islands, receptacles must be included. A two-height island offers a perfect backsplash location for receptacles.

An outlet strip that matches the trim color of the window offers a discreet, efficient solution to the question of where to put receptacles when there's no backsplash.

• pendants and chandeliers

Pendants and chandeliers are stylish and efficient ways to light an island, and they work just as well over kitchen dining surfaces. The options are many: a series of pendants, a single pendant with multiple secondary pendants, transparent and ribbed glass, colored acrylic—the sky's the limit.

Key concerns are ease of cleaning, height and width, and how the light appears to cooks and diners. As a rule, pendants are hung 30 in. above dining surfaces and 36 in. above work surfaces. Place wider fixtures higher up—from 40 in. to 48 in. above the workspace or table—so the fixture itself doesn't block the view and allows light to spread from this elevated vantage point. Translucent or transparent shades allow light to shine upward, too. This can help lift the apparent height of the ceiling.

Prevent glare by choosing a fixture with shielded, frosted, or deeply recessed bulbs. An opaque shade focuses attention on the table, while a translucent shade provides more ambient light. If a fancy pendant or chandelier is a dream but not yet in the budget, substitute a simple ceiling-mounted fixture.

ABOVE LEFT A custom-built, modern chandelier with recessed puck lights adds task lighting to the kitchen and makes the scale of the space more comfortable. Suspended blown-glass shades in scarlet provide decorative and ambient lighting.

ABOVE Three vibrant blown-glass fixtures with frosted incandescent bulbs hang over a large kitchen island to give task lighting a fun, decorative flair.

Task and ambient lighting comes from above in this Pacific Northwest kitchen. Two rows of recessed cans and two rows of suspended fixtures combine with sculptural fixtures to illuminate the space with style and variety.

• under, above, and inside: lighting cabinets

Undercabinet lighting is essential for working countertops, but it's also a great way to add ambient light throughout a kitchen. You might like the sparkle of undercabinet lights reflected on a polished countertop. Light-toned countertops and backsplashes boost the ability of undercabinet lights to brighten task space. For a softer look, select a honed, brushed, or matte countertop and backsplash, which diffuse reflected light.

There are four common types of undercabinet fixtures. Halogen puck lights give off bright white light, are easy to install, and generate quite a bit of heat. Fluorescent tubes are long lasting, energy efficient, and inexpensive. Xenon tubes last longer and generate less heat than halogen lights, and

have a warmer tint than fluorescent. LED (light-emitting diodes) lighting is expensive, but extremely long lasting and energy efficient.

Whatever the undercabinet light, avoid glare and reflection by installing fixtures on the bottom of wall cabinets, along the front inside edge. When added above wall cabinets, the same lighting fixtures add ambience and perceived spaciousness to a kitchen. And don't forget the inside of the cabinet: Add accent lighting to glass-paneled wall cabinets or door-operated task lighting to pantries and deep corner cabinets. Low-voltage fixtures such as rope lights, thin xenon tubes, and puck lights fit easily into small spaces, so every nook and cranny in the kitchen can be illuminated.

A deep skylight well showers this kitchen with direct sun at midday and diffuse light from dawn to dusk. Flush-mounted, low-voltage halogen fixtures provide task lighting.

Awning-style windows made of leaded stained glass add a delicate, artisanal touch to this elegant kitchen. The hints of color perfectly accord with the warm wood countertops and floor, copper sink and fittings, and incandescent cabinet lights.

Low-voltage halogen fixtures add sparkle to this custom-made Craftsman-style hutch. Glass shelves allow light to illuminate all the objects on display.

Pantry lights turn on when the
doors open, which makes it easy
to see what is on the shelves and
to read food labels or recipes.

ABOVE Frameless wall cabinets rest on a base that is thick enough to contain recessed halogen puck lights. The one-piece glass backsplash reflects the light from above and the sunlight from the outdoors.

BELOW Surface reflectivity makes a big difference in the surface finishes of backsplashes and countertops. Satin iridescent tile reflects light softly while polished granite is like a mirror.

all about...
BULBS

C oncern over energy use is changing the kitchen-lighting scene, primarily in terms of bulb type ("lamp" is the technical term). Incandescent bulbs (the standard light bulb) contain filaments and include tungsten. Halogens are more energy efficient and longer lasting than tungsten bulbs. Fluorescent and xenon bulbs, which contain gas, are also more efficient and last longer than incandescent bulbs. Xenon bulbs give off warmer light and more heat; fluorescent bulbs are more affordable.

Compact fluorescent lamps (CFLs) cost two to three times more than incandescent bulbs, but use 70 percent less energy and last 10 times longer. CFL color rendition has greatly improved recently; choose bulbs with a color temperature of 3,000 Kelvin or less for the warmest, most incandescent-like color.

Another low-energy fixture is the light-emitting diode (LED). LEDs are expensive but long lasting, use a minute amount of energy, and come in a variety of colors. Look to these for the future of kitchen lighting.

natural light

● ● ● BRING AS MUCH NATURAL LIGHT INTO YOUR KITCHEN AS POSSIBLE, AS THERE'S NOTHING LIKE IT FOR CHEERY AMBIENCE. Along with the obvious advantage of standing in for artificial fixtures, windows provide solar heat—overhangs and shades or curtains can moderate that—and offer ventilation to supplement a range hood. Windows should sit high enough to bounce light off the ceiling and can also stretch down close to the countertop level for task lighting. The ability to look beyond the walls of a kitchen helps enlarge its perceived size, and there may be a view out there that makes it worth forgoing exterior wall cabinets. An alternative is skylights, which boost brightness without taking up wall space; a deep well makes for a more diffuse light and reduces glaring sunlight.

A tall window abuts the sink and creates plenty of task lighting, but the in-line skylight bathes the entire kitchen in ambient light. Pendants and recessed fixtures make up the difference at night.

A high window sits above a single window in this kitchen. Both provide direct and reflected ambient and task lighting during the day. White walls enhance the brightness of the room.

ABOVE Warm light from suspended incandescent lights is balanced by the cooler-temperature daylight that comes in through skylights, which are recessed to provide diffused light and reduce shadows.

LEFT An artful arrangement of lighting brightens this kitchen from all angles. Awning windows offer an outdoor view and rainproof ventilation while light from the round window bounces off the ceiling. A single display cabinet is lit by a halogen puck light.

ABOVE A bay window is an unconventional, creative place for a pot rack. Just a few steps between the sink and range, pots are close at hand but not in the way.

LEFT A row of double-hung windows set off by wall-mounted lamps and framed drawings creates a formal rhythm in this renovated 19th-century farmhouse kitchen.

resources

Kitchens are a hugely popular subject, both in print and online. But where do you begin? To start, check the library and bookstores for books and magazines that feature the latest trends. Keep a file of ideas that appeal to you.

Where the Internet really shines as a resource for researching kitchens is giving you access to websites that show new products, compare costs, and, most importantly, give user advice. Tap into the experiences of people with experience—contractors, craftsmen, and designers. Visit product websites to get detailed information. There are also plenty of online forums where individuals, gather to share critiques, recommendations, and warnings about everything kitchen.

Here are the resources that I find helpful:

TAUNTON PRESS PUBLICATIONS

Taunton books and magazines offer the deepest and widest collection of information about home construction and interior design.

Visit taunton.com/books and click on "home design" or "kitchens" to find design and how-to information on kitchens and kitchen elements.

Pick up any issue of Fine Homebuilding to find at least one house design article, and don't pass up any of their special issues for in-depth info.

In the fall, look for Fine Homebuilding's Kitchens and Baths, an annual review of great projects and the latest information on appliances and materials. In the spring, check the newsstand or the Fine Homebuilding website for the annual Kitchen and Bath Planning Guide—a roundup of all the products and materials you need to get started on your new kitchen.

Fine Homebuilding and Fine Cooking magazines have websites that offer magazine articles for a subscription fee, plus free Web extras, such as articles and videos. Look for "Breaktime" at finehomebuilding.com and "Cookstalk" at finecooking.com.

BOOKS

Calloway, Stephen and Elizabeth Cromley (eds.), revised and updated by Alan Powers. *The Elements of Style: An Encyclopedia of Domestic Architectural Detail.* Ontario: Firefly Books, 2005.
An excellent, heavily illustrated guide for researching hardware, trim, lighting, flooring, and wallpaper styles for a period kitchen.

McAlester, Virginia and Lee. *A Field Guide to American Houses.* New York: Alfred Knopf, 1984.
This 20-plus-year-old book is still the best guide to American house styles.

WEB SITES

aarp.org/families/home_design/kitchen/
For design tips to make kitchens more useful and accessible.

aham.org
The Association of Home Appliance Manufacturers' consumer pages offer archived articles, news, advice, and links to home appliance manufacturer pages.

appliancist.com
This online magazine is dedicated to the latest in home appliances and related trends.

bestgreenblogs.com
Best Green Blogs is a directory of blogs that focus on green issues and sustainability.

buildinggreen.com
This is an independent company that educates building-industry professionals about how to improve the environmental performance of building.

chowhound.com
Not just about food, this website offers plenty of opinions about the room where food gets cooked.

consumerreports.org
There's a fair amount you can see here for free: text about countertop materials, installation, and upkeep, blogs, product videos, and forums, but only subscribers can view detailed review charts.

energystar.gov
This easy-to-navigate website is packed with information on how to build and live more efficiently. The program also reviews and rates appliances.

hgtv.com
Click on "kitchens" for a wealth of video clips about featured kitchens.

lfloor.com/articles
This floor-seller has a library of articles on flooring types and recommendations on how to choose the right floor for you.

materialicio.us
This blog focuses on residential architecture, design, craftsmanship, materials, and products.

nari.org
The driving force of the National Association of the Remodeling Industry (NARI) is to advance and promote the remodeling industry's professionalism, products, and public purpose.

nkba.org
The National Kitchen & Bath Association (NKBA) website offers consumers information on appliance news and on how to find a kitchen designer.

ths.gardenweb.com/forums/
On this site, look specifically for the Kitchen and Appliance forums. They are loaded with discussions, links, and photos of everything involving kitchens.

finishedkitchens.blogspot.com
A treasure trove of kitchen photos, all tagged with keywords for easy searching of products and materials.

thekitchendesigner.org/journal/
This is the blog of kitchen designer Susan Serra, an enthusiastic purveyor of kitchen-design ideas and materials.

photo credits

pp. ii-iii: Photo © Susan Gilmore, Design: Rehkamp Larson Architects, Inc.; pp. vi–1: (photo 1) Photo © Scot Zimmerman, Design: Vickee Byrum; (photo 2) Photo © James West, Design: Tonic Design; (photo 3) Photo © Susan Gilmore, Design: Rehkamp Larson Architects, Inc.; (photo 4) Photo © Olson Photographic LLC; (photo 5) Photo © Huyla Kolabas, Design: Beinfeld Architecture with Christopher Peacock Cabinetry; (photo 6) Photo © Eric Roth, Design: Gerald Pomery Design Group; (photo 7) Photo © davidduncanlivingston.com; (photo 8) Photo © Olson Photographic LLC, Design: Sebastian Carpenter Design; pp. 2–3: (left) Photo © Huyla Kolabas; (middle) Photo © Randy O'Rourke; (right) Photo © Olson Photographic LLC, Design: Marc Lindsell Architecture

CHAPTER 1

p. 4: Photo © davidduncanlivingston.com; Design: Erica Broberg, Smith River Kitchens

p. 6: Photo © davidduncanlivingston

p. 7: Photo © Hulya Kolabas; Design: Deborah Emory, Emory Design Associates

p. 8: (top) Photo © Eric Roth; (bottom) Photo © Hulya Kolabas; Design: Beinfield Architecture PC with Christopher Peacock Cabinetry

p 9: Photo © James West; Design: Dixon Weinstein Architects

p. 10 © Photo: James West

p. 11: (top) Photo © Scot Zimmerman; (bottom) Photo © Olson Photographic LLC; Design: General Woodcraft

p. 12: Photo © James R. Salomon

p. 13: (left) Photo © Olson Photographic LLC; (top right) Photo © Scot Zimmerman; Design: InStyle and Rail Kitchen Designs, (bottom right): Photo © Olson Photographic LLC

p. 14: Photo © Hulya Kolabas

p. 15: (top) Photo © Eric Roth; Design: Trikeenan Tileworks; (bottom) Design: Morse Construction; (right) Photo © Eric Roth; Gleysteen Design LLC

p. 16: Photo © davidduncanlivingston.com; Design: Erica Broberg, Smith River Kitchens

p. 17: (right) Photo © davidduncanlivingston. com; (bottom) Photo © Scot Zimmerman Design: Vickee Byrum, Yellow Door Design

p. 18: Photo © davidduncanlivingston.com

p. 19: Photo © Eric Roth, Design: Susan Sargent Design

p. 20: (left) Photo © Brian Vanden Brink Design: Polshek Partnership Architects; (right) Photo © Scot Zimmerman Design: Ann Marie Barton, AMB Design

p. 21: Photo © davidduncanlivingston.com

p. 22: Photo © Olson Photographic LLC, Design: Legacy Development

p. 23: (top) Photo © Ken Gutmaker, Design: Ross Levy, 10d.com; (bottom) Photo © Brian Vanden Brink, Design: Group 3 Architects

p. 24: Photo © Olson Photographic LLC, Design: Jody Fierz

p. 25: (top) Photo © Hulya Kolabas, Design: Deborah Emory, Emory Design Associates, (bottom) Photo © Olson Photographic LLC, Design: Cucina Design

p. 26: Photo © Randy O'Rourke, Design: Leah Lenney Interiors, Larchmont, NY

p. 27: Photo © Storybook Studios

p. 28: Photo © Randy O'Rourke, Design: Kaehler Moore Architects

p. 29: (left) Photo by Daniel Morrison, courtesy *Fine Homebuilding,* © The Taunton Press, Inc., Design: Sarah Farrell, Moore Architects; (right) Photo © Dan Rockhill, Design: Dan Rockhill+ Associates

p. 30: Photo © Randy O'Rourke, Design: Kaehler Moore Architects

p. 31: (left): Photo © Ken Gutmaker; Design: Deliberate Design + Architecture; (top right) Photo © James West, Design: Tonic Design; (bottom right) Photo © Hulya Kolabas, Design: Deborah Emory, Emory Design Associates

p. 32: (left) Photo © Olson Photographic LLC, Design: Amazing Spaces; (right) Photo © Eric Roth, Design: Jonathan Poore

p. 33: Photo © davidduncanlivingston.com, Design: Jean Larette Interior Design

p. 34: (top) Photo © Eric Roth; (bottom) Photo by Melissa Harris, courtesy *Fine Homebuilding,* © The Taunton Press, Inc., Design: Melissa Harris

p. 35: Photo © James R. Salomon

p. 36: Photo by Charles Miller, courtesy *Fine Homebuilding,* © The Taunton Press, Inc., Design: Prentiss Architects

p. 37: (left) Photo © Ken Gutmaker, Design: Starkweather Bondy Architects; (right) Photo by Charles Miller, courtesy *Fine Homebuilding,* © The Taunton Press, Inc., Design: Street, Lundgren and Foster, Architects

CHAPTER 2

p. 38: Photo © Hulya Kolabas, Design: Beinfield Architecture PC with Christopher Peacock Cabinetry,

p. 40: (left) Photo © James West, Design: Dixon Weinstein Architects; (right) Photo © Ken Gutmaker, Design: Cunningham Designs

p. 41: (top) Photo © James West, Design: Dixon Weinstein Architects; (bottom) Photo

© Ken Gutmaker, Design: Dirk Stennick Design, Construction: Alward Construction

p. 42: Photo © davidduncanlivingston.com

p. 43: (left) Photo © Hulya Kolabas; (top right) Photo © James West, Design: Tonic Design; (bottom right) Photo © Brian Vanden Brink, Design: Elliott Elliott Norelius Architecture

p. 44: Photo © davidduncanlivingston.com, Design: Erica Broberg, Smith River Kitchens

p. 45: (left) Photo © Ken Gutmaker, Design: Rocky and Marie Kleinrock and Redhorse Constructors; (right) Photo © Olson Photographic LLC, Design: Amazing Spaces

p. 46: (left) Photo © Randy O'Rourke, Design: Hamady Architects with Dale and James Gould; (right) Photo © Scot Zimmerman, Design: Gulch Design Group

p. 47: Photo © Susan Gilmore, Design: Rehkamp Larson Architects, Inc.

p. 48: Photo © Brian Vanden Brink, Design: John Colamarino

p. 49: Photo © Randy O'Rourke, Design: Kaehler Moore Architects

p. 50: (left) Photo © Olson Photographic LLC, Design: Mark Brady Kitchens; (right) Photo © James R. Salomon

p. 51: Photo © James West, Design: Tonic Design

CHAPTER 3

p. 52: Photo © Hulya Kolabas, Design: Deborah Emory, Emory Design Associates

p. 54: Photo © Randy O'Rourke, Design: Susan Anderson

p. 55: (top) Photo © Randy O'Rourke, Design: Hamady Architects with Dale and James Gould; (bottom left) Photo © Olson Photographic LLC, Design: Amazing Spaces; (bottom right) Photo © Ken Gutmaker, Design: Marc Lindsell Architecture

p. 56: (left) Photo © Brian Vanden Brink Design: Elliott Elliott Norelius Architecture; (right) Photo © Randy O'Rourke Design: Roc Caivano Architects

p. 57: (top) Photo © Ken Gutmaker, Design: Rocky and Marie Kleinrock and Redhorse Constructors; (bottom) Photo © Ken Gutmaker, Design: Deliberate Design + Architecture

p. 58: Photo © Olson Photographic LLC, Design: Elm City Architects

p. 59: (top) Photo © Eric Roth, Design: Heidi Pribell Interior Design; (bottom) Photo by Brian Vanden Brink, courtesy *Fine Homebuilding,* © The Taunton Press, Inc.

p. 60: Photo © James West Design: Dixon Weinstein Architects

p. 61: (left) Photo © Susan Gilmore, Design: Rehkamp Larson Architects, Inc.; (right) Photo © Brian Vanden Brink, Hutker Architects

p. 62: Photo © Ken Gutmaker, Design: Marc Lindsell Architecture

p. 63: Photo by Brian Pontolilo, courtesy *Fine Homebuilding,* © The Taunton Press, Inc., Design: Peregrine Design/Build

p. 64: Photo © Ken Gutmaker, Design: Deliberate Design + Architecture

p. 65: (top) Photo © James West, Design: Dixon Weinstein Architects; (bottom left) Photo © Scot Zimmerman, Design: Bruce Taylor, Summit Design; (right) Photo and Design by John Nourbakhsh and Toby Witte (Dialect Design), courtesy *Fine Homebuilding,* © The Taunton Press, Inc.

p. 66: (top) Photo © Olson Photographic LLC Design: Kitchen and Bath Design by Betsy House; (bottom) Photo © Derrill Bazzy, Design: South Mountain Company

p. 67: (top) Photo © Olson Photographic LLC Design: Nautilus Architects; (bottom) Photo © James West, Design: Tonic Design

p. 68: (left) Photo © Brian Vanden Brink, Design: Catalano Architects; (top right) Photo by Charles Miller, courtesy *Fine Homebuilding,* © The Taunton Press, Inc., Design: David Edrington Architect; (bottom right) Photo © Randy O'Rourke, Design: Hudson Valley Preservation

p. 69: Photo © Ken Gutmaker, Design: Dirk Stennick Design, Construction: Alward Construction

p. 70: (left) Photo by Brian Pontolilo, courtesy *Fine Homebuilding,* © The Taunton Press, Inc., Design: Peregrine Design/Build; (top right) Photo © Susan Gilmore, Design: Rehkamp Larson Architects, Inc.; (bottom right) Photo © Susan Gilmore, Design: Rehkamp Larson Architects, Inc.

p. 71: Photo © davidduncanlivingston.com

p. 72: Photo © Ken Gutmaker, Design: Starkweather Bondy Architecture

p. 73: (top) Photo © Ken Gutmaker, Design: Lucy Penfield, Lucy Interior Design; (bottom) Photo © davidduncanlivingston.com

CHAPTER 4

p. 74: Photo © Randy O'Rourke, Design: Kaehler Moore Architects

p. 76: Photo © Olson Photographic LLC

p. 77: (top left) Photo © Hulya Kolabas; (top right) Photo © Randy O'Rourke, Design: Kaehler Moore Architects; (bottom) Photo © Ken Gutmaker Rehkamp Larson Architects, Inc.

p. 78: (left) Photo © Ken Gutmaker, Design: Dirk Stennick Design, Construction: Alward Construction; (right) Photo © Ken Gutmaker, Design: Deliberate Design + Architecture

p. 79: (top) Photo © Eric Roth; (bottom left) Photo © Olson Photographic LLC; (bottom right) Photo © davidduncanlivingston.com Design: Backen Gillam Architects with Nicole Hollis

p. 80: Photo © Randy O'Rourke, Design: Susan Anderson and Jim Jamieson, architect

p. 81: (top) Photo © Randy O'Rourke, Design: Kaehler Moore Architects; (bottom left) Photo by Storybook Studios courtesy *Fine Homebuilding,* © The Taunton Press, Inc.; (right) Photo by Roe A. Osborn, courtesy *Fine Homebuilding,* © The Taunton Press, Inc., Design: Carolyn Murray, Heritage Design Group

p. 82: Photo © Susan Gilmore, Design: Rehkamp Larson Architects, Inc.

p. 83: (left) Photo © James West Design: Dixon Weinstein Architects; (top right) Photo © Susan Gilmore, Design: Rehkamp Larson Architects, Inc.; (bottom right): Photo © Ken Gutmaker, Design: Dirk Stennick Design, Construction: Alward Construction

p. 84: (left) Photo © Hulya Kolabas, Design: Deborah Emory, Emory Design Associates; (top right) Photo © James West Design: Dixon Weinstein Architects

p. 85: Photo © Randy O'Rourke, Design: Hudson Valley Preservation

p. 86: Photo © Randy O'Rourke, Design: Kent Kitchen Works

p. 88: (left) Photo © Scot Zimmerman; (top right) Photo © Hulya Kolabas, Design: Beinfield Architecture PC with Christopher Peacock Cabinetry; (bottom right) Photo © davidduncanlivingston.com

p. 89: (top left) Photo © davidduncanlivingston.com; (bottom left) Photo © Scot Zimmerman, Design: Ann Marie Barton, AMB Design; (right) Photo © Scot Zimmerman, Design: Bruce Taylor, Summit Design

p. 90: Photo © Ken Gutmaker, Design: Davids Killory Architecture, Construction: Alward Construction

p. 91: (top left) Photo by Chris Ermides, courtesy *Fine Homebuilding,* © The Taunton Press, Inc., Design: WMS Construction; (bottom left) Photo © Olson Photographic LLC, Design: Candlelight Cabinetry; (top right) Photo © Randy O'Rourke Design: Kent Kitchen Works

p. 92: Photo courtesy Kraftmaid

p. 93: (top and bottom left) Photo © Randy O'Rourke, Design: Susan Anderson and Jim Jamieson, architect; (top right) Photo © davidduncanlivingston.com, Design: Arclinea San Francisco; (bottom right) Photo © Scot Zimmerman, Design: Lisman Studio

p. 94: (top) Photo © James West, Design: Tonic Design; (bottom) Photo © Tria Giovan

p. 95: (left) Photo © Scot Zimmerman, Design: Bruce Taylor, Summit Design; (right) Photo courtesy Kraftmaid

p. 96: Photo by Charles Miller, courtesy *Fine Homebuilding,* © The Taunton Press, Inc., Design: Kraftmaid

p. 97: (top left) Photo © James West, Design: Dixon Weinstein Architects; (top right) Photo © davidduncanlivingston.com; (bottom) Photo courtesy Kraftmaid

p. 98: Photo by Charles Miller, courtesy *Fine Homebuilding,* © The Taunton Press, Inc., Design: Armstrong

p. 99: (left) Photo by Brian Pontolilo, courtesy *Fine Homebuilding,* © The Taunton Press, Inc., Design: Dana Moore; (top right) Photo courtesy Yorktowne Cabinetry; (bottom right) Photo by Charles Miller, courtesy *Fine Homebuilding,* © The Taunton Press, Inc., Design: DeWils

p. 100: (left) Photo © Ken Gutmaker, Design: Davids Killory Architecture, Construction: Alward Construction; (right) Photo © James West, Design: Dixon Weinstein Architects

p. 101: Photo © Hulya Kolabas, Design: Beinfield Architecture PC with Christopher Peacock Cabinetry

p. 102: (left) Photo © Scot Zimmerman, Design: InStyle and Rail Kitchen Designs; (right) Photo by Charles Bickford, courtesy *Fine Homebuilding,* © The Taunton Press, Inc. Design: Joel Wheeler

p. 103: (top) Photo © Randy O'Rourke, Design: Kent Kitchen Works; (bottom) Photo © Randy O'Rourke, Design: Hamady Architects with Dale and James Gould

p. 104: (top) Photo © James West, Design: Tonic Design; (bottom) Photo by Roe A. Osborn, courtesy *Fine Homebuilding,* © The Taunton Press, Inc., Design: Carolyn Murray, Heritage Design Group

p. 105: (top) Photo © davidduncanlivingston.com; (bottom) Photo © Randy O'Rourke, Design: Susan Anderson and Jim Jamieson, architect

p. 106: Photo © Derrill Bazzy, Design: South Mountain Company

p. 107: (left) Photo © Ken Gutmaker, Design: Lucy Penfield, Lucy Interior Design; (top right) Photo © davidduncanlivingston.com, Design: Erica Broberg, Smith River Kitchens; (bottom right) Photo © Scot Zimmerman, Design: Hillary Reed, HRI Design

p. 108: Photo © Dan Rockhill, Design: Dan Rockhill+Associates

p. 109: (bottom left) Photo © Randy O'Rourke, Design: Kaehler Moore Architects; (bottom right) Photo © Ken Gutmaker, Design: Davids Killory Architecture, Construction: Alward Construction

p. 110: Photo © Hulya Kolabas, Design: Deborah Emory, Emory Design Associates

p. 111: (top) Photo courtesy Kraftmaid; (bottom) Photo © Randy O'Rourke, Design: Kaehler Moore Architects

p. 112: Photo © Hulya Kolabas

p. 169: Photo © Eric Roth, Design: Gerald Pomeroy Design Group

p. 170: Photo by Charles Miller, courtesy *Fine Homebuilding,* © The Taunton Press, Inc., Design: Street, Lundgren and Foster, Architects

p. 171: (left) Photo: Eric Roth, Design: Soane Interieurs; (top right) Photo © Olson Photographic LLC, Design: Kitchen and Bath Design Creations; (bottom right) Photo © Ken Gutmaker Design: Davids Killory Architecture, Construction: Alward Construction

p. 172: Photo © Eric Roth

p. 173: (top) Photo © James West, Design: Dixon Weinstein Architects; (bottom) Photo © Ken Gutmaker, Design: Davids Killory Architecture, Construction: Alward Construction

p. 174: (top) Photo © James West, Design: Tonic Design; (bottom left) Photo by Charles Miller, courtesy *Fine Homebuilding,* © The Taunton Press, Inc., Design: John Hurst; (bottom right) Photo © Randy O'Rourke, Design: Kaehler Moore Architects

p. 175: (top) Photo © James R. Salomon; (bottom) Photo © Randy O'Rourke, Design: Susan Anderson and Jim Jamieson, architect

p. 176: (top) Photo © Scot Zimmerman, Design: Lisman Studio; (bottom) Photo © James West, Design: Tonic Design, Concrete design and production: Meld USA

p. 177: (top) Photo courtesy General Electric; (bottom) Photo © davidduncanlivingston.com

p. 178: Photo © davidduncanlivingston.com, Design: Wolf

p. 179: Photo © Eric Roth

p. 180: (left) Photo © Scot Zimmerman, Design: Lisman Studio; (right) Photo © Eric Roth, Design: Paul D. Laffey

p. 181: Photo © Eric Roth

p. 182: Photo © Randy O'Rourke, Design: Susan Anderson and Jim Jamieson, architect

p. 183: (left) Photo © Hulya Kolabas; (top right) Photo © James West Design: Dixon Weinstein Architects; (bottom right) Photo © Hulya Kolabas Design: Deborah Emory, Emory Design Associates

CHAPTER 8

p. 184: Photo by Roe A. Osborn, courtesy *Fine Homebuilding,* © The Taunton Press, Inc., Design: Du Charme Architecture

p. 186: Photo © Olson Photographic LLC, Design: Joe Cugno Architects

p. 187: (left) Photo © Hulya Kolabas, Design: Deborah Emory, Emory Design Associates; (right) Photo © Eric Roth, Design: Horst Buchanan Architects

p. 188: Photo © Ken Gutmaker, Design: Deliberate Design + Architecture

p. 189: (top left) Photo © Olson Photographic LLC, Design: Amazing Spaces; (bottom left)

Photo © Randy O'Rourke, Design: Susan Anderson and Jim Jamieson, architect; (bottom right) Photo courtesy Teragren Bamboo

p. 190: Photo © Eric Roth, Design: Leslie Fine Interiors

p. 191: (left) Photo © Derrill Bazzy, Design: South Mountain Company; (top right) Photo © Hulya Kolabas, Design: Deborah Emory, Emory Design Associates; (bottom right) Photo: Eric Roth, Design: Rehkamp Larson Architects

p. 192: (left) Photo © Eric Roth, Design: Albert, Righter & Tittman Architects; (right) Photo © Olson Photographic LLC, Design: Prentiss Architects, Inc.

p. 194: (left) Photo © Olson Photographic LLC, Design: Amazing Spaces; (right) Photo © davidduncanlivingston.com

p. 195: (top) Photo © Eric Roth, Design: Joseph Kennard Architects; (bottom left) Photo © davidduncanlivingston.com; (right) Photo © Ken Gutmaker, Design: Deliberate Design + Architecture

CHAPTER 9

p. 196: Photo © Ken Gutmaker, Design: Rehkamp Larson Architects

p. 198: Photo © Eric Roth

p. 199: Photo © Randy O'Rourke, Design: Kaehler Moore Architects

p. 200: Photo © James West, Design: Tonic Design

p. 201: (top): Photo © Ken Gutmaker, Design: Davids Killory Architects, Builder: Alward Construction; (bottom) Photo © Randy O'Rourke, Design: Kaehler Moore Architects

pp. 202-3: (left) Photo © Eric Roth; (center) Photo © Olson Photographic LLC, Design: Acorn Cabinetry; (right) Photo © James West, Design: Dixon Weinstein Architects

pp. 204-5: (left) Photo © Hulya Kolabas, Design: Deborah Emory, Emory Design Associates; (center) Photo © Ken Gutmaker Design: Dirk Stennick Design, Construction: Alward Construction; (right) Photo © Charles Miller, Design: Geoffrey Prentiss

p. 206: Photo by Brian Pontolilo, courtesy *Fine Homebuilding,* © The Taunton Press, Inc., Design: John O'Connor, Basis Design Build

p. 207: (left) Photo © Eric Roth; (right) Photo by Chris Greene courtesy *Fine Homebuilding,* © The Taunton Press, Inc., Design: Rex Alexander Brethren

p. 208: Photo © Randy O'Rourke, Design: Hamady Architects with Dale and James Gould

p. 209: (top) Photo © Randy O'Rourke, Design: Kaehler Moore Architects; (bottom) Photo © Eric Roth Design: Sebastian Carpenter Design

p. 210: Photo © James West, Design: Dixon Weinstein Architects

p. 211: (top) Photo © Ken Gutmaker, Design: Starkweather Bondy Architects; (left) Photo: Charles Bickford, courtesy *Fine Homebuilding,* © The Taunton Press, Inc., Design: Greene & Proppe; (right) Photo © James West, Design: Tonic Design

pp. 212-213: Photo © Randy O'Rourke, Design: Hamady Architects with Dale and James Gould; (right) Photo © Ken Gutmaker, Design: Rock and Marie Kleinrock and Redhorse Constructors,